GW00787963

Write it, Gig it, Sell it, Make it!

Ben Keep

ISBN-13: 978-1519495662

ISBN-10: 1519495668

Dedicated to

James 'Nortee' Norton 1977 - 2000

Cujo 1997 - 2007

CONTENTS

	Acknowledgments	i
1	Introduction	1
2	Starting a band	7
3	Rehearsing	15
4	Writing songs	23
5	Writing lyrics	30
6	Recording	34
7	Home recording	44
8	Designing your album	46
9	Gig preparation and set-up	69
10	Playing live	74
11	Promoting gigs	80
12	Writing a biography	91
13	Writing a press release	101
14	Building your brand	105
15	Building a website	111
16	Digital Marketing	121
17	Automation	129
18	Blogging	132
19	Exposure	137
20	Networking	143
21	Releasing music	147
22	Marketing plan	152
23	Conclusion	161
24	Guitar set-up	163

ACKNOWLEDGMENTS

I would like to express my gratitude to my wife Tertia Keep for assisting me in the proof reading and editing of this book. My thanks also to my friends Kevin Dawson, Jamie Hook, Will Anderson, Mark Beaumont, Brian Nash, Tim Hamill, Willie Scott, and Vince Cooper who have allowed me to include their names and our stories.

INTRODUCTION

Do you want to be a successful band or artist, with awesome tunes that are played on the radio, in clubs and on stereos and smart phones all over the world? Whose gigs are packed with fans dancing and shouting your lyrics back at you, a band that actually makes money?

Well I can't write your songs for you, but what I can do is pass on all the knowledge from my experiences to help you be successful.

So who am I, and why do I know what I'm talking about? And if I do know what I'm talking about, then why am I not in a massive rock band selling millions of albums?

Well I'll explain.

I have been playing in bands for over twenty years, some

originals bands, and some cover bands, sometimes three or four bands at the same time. I'm an experienced band manager, event organiser, event promoter, lead vocalist, backing singer, lead guitarist, rhythm guitarist, bassist, songwriter and producer.

During my musical career I have played over 1000 gigs, from solo acoustic gigs in small bars to headlining festival stages. Roughly 200 of these gigs I organised and promoted myself or with my band and quite often stage-managed and sound-engineered as well.

I have co-written, recorded and produced 10 albums, designed numerous album and single covers, websites and hundreds of flyers and posters. I've also had the privilege of working with many very talented and experienced people.

The majority of my experience, which I will often be referring to in this book, is acquired from the ten years I spent in a popular unsigned/indie London three piece rock band called Cujo. In Cujo we did a lot of great things that were very successful, but we also made mistakes.

As we work our way through the chapters I will be sharing some of these stories so you can replicate the good bits, and avoid making some of the silly mistakes we did.

Whilst I spent every evening, weekend and holiday working as a musician; during the daytimes I built a successful career in sales and marketing, specialising in digital marketing.

I am now the Consulting Manager for a successful Management Consultancy but I still work very closely with and manage the Marketing team, actively keeping up with all the current marketing trends, tools and software.

I'm getting dangerously close to my fortieth birthday and the chance of me starting another band are getting slim, but If I could jump into a Plutonium powered DeLorean, set the time circuits to 1995 and go back and start a band again with the knowledge I have now, I'm pretty sure we could be that band on the cover of the NME, play-listed on RadioX and headlining the Reading and Leads Festival.

But Plutonium is hard to come by in Kent so that's not going to happen any time soon. So in fifty years' time, I'm probably not going to be remembered for the songs I've written or the band I play in. So by writing this book I can help others achieve that goal and some of you might remember me for that book I wrote!

When I first started playing in a band, I, like many of my mates thought all you had to do was write some cool tunes, play a gig and invite a few record companies along, they would love the gig then sign you up to a massive record deal. Then next thing you know, you're Top of the Pops, rich and famous!

Well, unfortunately it doesn't work like that, especially these days when there is so much talent out there. Record companies now want to see that you already have a great brand with a big following and some great recorded material before they will even consider signing you. With so many artists producing and selling their own music, and apps like Spotify and Apple streaming music, the record companies just don't make as much money as they used to, so they are very careful where they spend it.

The good news is; these days you don't need a record company, you can do everything yourselves for not a lot of money. This book will teach you how to do that. I'm going to cover a number of subjects from starting a band, rehearsing, writing, gigging, marketing and selling your music.

It's January 2016 now and this book will have a sell by date. Most of the text will remain very relevant: starting a band, rehearsing, gigging, recording etc. but digital marketing is constantly changing. If I wrote this book ten years ago I would be telling you all about Myspace, how to build your page, which clever tools to use to get thousands of friends, how to use HTML to create clever automated adverts that pop onto everyone's timelines, and lots of other cool stuff. But as you know, Myspace isn't that popular anymore, which is a real shame as it was a brilliant platform for artists and bands.

Currently everyone is using Facebook, Twitter, LinkedIn, and Instagram, and all the other new exciting websites and apps, but who knows what we will all be doing this time next year or the year after. Will Google+ become the most popular? Will Apple bring out their own social media platform and take over the world?! Who knows!

So that is why this book has a sell by date. By the end of 2016 or mid 2017 there will be loads more digital platforms and marketing tools out there, and so some of the information I teach you in this book will be out of date. So I will re-write an updated version every year.

After you have read this book, I would love to hear your feedback. Is there anything you think is interesting that I have not covered, or not gone into enough detail about? Are there any new marketing tools I have not mentioned that you think are worth mentioning?

If you have anything to say, please visit the website www.wgsm.co.uk and get in touch. If your suggestion is included in the next version I will reference you at the end of the book.

STARTING A BAND

I first started playing guitar at the age of nine with a few lessons from my father and a few lessons at school, but I was never very good. I wasn't interested in learning scales or weird difficult-to-play chords, or practicing any of the songs the teacher had chosen for us to learn.

At the age of fourteen that all changed. It was 1991 and into the charts came some of the best classic rock singles of all time. Nirvana - Smells Like Teen Spirit, Metallica - Enter Sandman, Guns & Roses - Live and Let Die, Pearl Jam - Alive and Red Hot Chilli Peppers - Under the Bridge: and I was hooked!

I knew I needed to be in a rock band! I bought a budget Fender Sun Mustang guitar, a cheap amp and the Nirvana, Metallica and Guns and Roses guitar tablature books. I didn't buy proper music books as I never actually learnt how to read music.

A year later with the ability to play power chords and a few simple solos, I was ready to start a band!

To be a good musician you need to be able to play your instrument very well, but it's not essential to have studied music and know all the weird and wonderful chords and scales to start a band. Playing in a band is much more than being a musician, it's getting together with likeminded mates and having a good time, becoming a kind of musical family. You learn from each other, learn how each of you play, your strengths and weaknesses and develop your own unique sound. Over time you will gel together like a well-oiled machine, developing a tight sound that is your own.

You will spend a lot of time with the people in your band and after a while you will become very close.

I played in a few bands when I was 16 – 17, nothing very serious, just mates having fun, doing the odd gig in a church hall or school assembly. When I turned 18 I got a job in a local pub, The Rose & Crown in Enfield. A week later a guy called Kevin Dawson also started work at the pub. Kevin, like me, wore grungy clothes, had a Kurt Cobain style haircut, played guitar and listened to all the same bands I did. So obviously we hit it off straight away. After a few weeks we decided to start a band. Kevin knew a drummer, I knew a bassist, so we booked a studio and we were off. Unfortunately the drummer and bassist were not as committed to the band as Kevin and me, so over the next six months we rehearsed about once a month, wrote a few songs, did a couple of gigs; but we weren't really getting anywhere. The drummer eventually quit and the bassist went away to University. We then enrolled another couple of mates, who had both just left other bands; Jamie Hook on the Drums and James Norton on the bass. Jamie and James were both awesome musicians and like Kevin and me, they were both passionate about creating a brilliant and successful rock band. Cujo was born!

We started rehearsing every week, writing new songs every week, gigging once or twice a month and hanging out in-between. As you can imagine, spending that much time with each other, we all became very good mates and very close.

Cujo, as a four piece, continued writing and gigging and getting more and more popular for the next four years. Sadly on July 14th 2000, tragedy struck. James Norton was killed in a motorbike accident on his way home from work.

This hit us all hard, not only had we lost our bassist, and a very good one too, we also lost a very close friend. A friend who we had spent two or three days a week with over the past four years, a friend who was part of our dreams to be a successful band.

For a while we said Cujo was over, there was no Cujo without James. After a few months, we realised that James wouldn't have wanted us to quit, so we decided to audition for a new bassist. We found a bassist, he had everything we needed: he was a friend of ours, someone we could trust, he liked the same music, was a very good bassist and very keen to be in our band. We invited him along to a couple of rehearsals and even though he played the songs very well, the songs just didn't feel or sound the same, and playing with a different bassist in the rehearsal room didn't feel right either. So in the end we decided not to replace James with another bassist but to become a three piece. I bought myself a bass guitar and a bass amp and we re-arranged all our songs so they could be played without a rhythm guitar.

After a while we started sounding great again and now with an extra reason to be successful, we were doing it for James.

So that's how Cujo started and I think a good example of how a band can become such a close-knit unit

So how do you start your own band?

Perhaps you already have a full line-up of mates with a similar taste in music and similar aspirations for starting a band, then that's great - you're ready to hit the rehearsal rooms.

But if you need band members, then you need to go and find some. There are plenty of websites you can advertise free of charge like joinmyband or join-a-band. You may even find one local to your town or county.

On these websites there is usually two types of adverts: bands looking for musicians, or musicians looking for bands. Have a look through all the musicians who have advertised themselves, and you can place an advert yourself.

When writing your advert, there are a few things you need to include. You need to explain what type of musicians you are looking for, where you are based, and tell them a bit about your music style, musical inspirations and plans. Ask any interested people to get in touch by email and also send any demo's, if they have any. Your advert might look something like this;

Male or Female drummer and bass player wanted for a new start-up originals rock band in Northampton.

Preferably aged between sixteen and twenty.

Inspirations include: The Arctic Monkeys, Reverend and The Makers and Miles Cane.

Get in touch and send any demo's to 'Your Email address' or call 'Your Name' on 'Your Mobile Number'.

Hopefully you will get a few replies to your advert.

When people do apply, have a chat with them over email, listen to any material they might have sent you. Don't just tell someone they are in your band straight away.

Make sure you have vetted them, speak to them on the phone, perhaps meet up for a beer, and introduce them to the rest of the band, if you already have other members. You're going to spend a lot of time with this person so you need to make sure you get on and that you can trust them.

You need to audition new members. The last thing you want is to is invite someone to be in your band before you hear them play, then find out during rehearsals that they are rubbish and you have to fire them.

Auditions can be quite informal, just invite them along to a rehearsal room for a jam. If you have a few people who are potential candidates for the role, you could book a rehearsal room for a few hours and ask them all to come along at different times to audition. Give them a couple of songs to learn which you will all play at the audition; by doing this you get to hear how each of them play the same songs, so it's easier to compare them, but also to see who made the effort and learnt the songs properly. If they don't bother learning them properly, then they're probably not the right person for the job.

Try and find people who live local to you. You are going to want to rehearse quite regularly and no-one will want to spend too much time and money traveling to rehearsals.

Once you have your line up, there are a couple of things you should probably discuss. How much time you are prepared to put into the band, do you all want to be rehearsing once a week and maybe gigging once a month? And how much money are you prepared to put into the band and how are you are going to split any money you make? It's best to get this agreed early on as you don't want to get into arguments further down the line after you've all put a lot of time and money into creating a band.

In my opinion, you should split all money evenly between all the band members. If you look at some of the big bands that have been going for many years, and the ones who have split up, quite often the reason is financial disagreements. The bands who stay together for a long time are typically the ones who split the money evenly between them.

In Cujo we split everything equally. We didn't very often pay ourselves any money, instead we paid the money we earned into a band bank account. We used that money for things like rehearsals, recordings, flyer, posters etc.

It costs money to be in a band (quite a lot of money if you break cymbals at the rate our drummer did!). You have to buy instruments, new guitar strings, new drum skins, rehearsal room hire, transport, drinks, etc. When you are all paying these costs, then why should one of you take more money than the rest?

Do you need a Manager? Not yet as you can do most things yourselves with a little help from this book. But if you have someone you can trust who's willing to do it for free, someone you believe would be a good manager, then why not?

When you start doing things like booking tours and dealing with legal contracts then maybe think about a professional management. Managers typically charge you 10% of your profits. So if you don't need one, then don't bother.

REHEARSING

If you don't already have a local rehearsal room you use or know about, get on Google and find one. Most decent studios have websites or have listed themselves online somewhere.

Give them a call and find out what facilities they have, what equipment is available in the rooms and the cost. Rehearsal rooms don't tend to cost very much, roughly £10-£15 per hour.

Book a room for three or four hours and split the cost between you. If you are booking a rehearsal room to audition people, you can't really charge the people coming for auditions, so for this session you and anyone else already in your band should pay.

Most studios will have a PA, microphones and microphone stands. Some studios have drum kits and instrument amps for people to use. Usually the microphones and PA hire are included in the studio cost, but if you want to hire drums or amps, then this might cost a little more. You will definitely need to take your own instruments, cymbals, snare and drum sticks.

Setting up your equipment takes time, time which you are paying for, so the quicker you get set up and ready to start playing the better. For this reason, to save time, I always prefer to use whatever equipment they have available. It doesn't matter if it's not the best equipment in the world, as long as you get a pretty good sound that's all you need to rehearse.

You will probably have to plug the microphones in and set the sound for the vocals. If you aren't sure how to do this ask someone at the rehearsal studio to show you. They will be more than happy to help because if you do something wrong, you could blow their PA system! PA systems are pretty hard to blow with just vocals going in, but if you are plugging instruments and amps into it, you have to be a bit careful as to how loud you have it.

Once you have set everything up, its good practice to jam for a bit to get the volumes sounding right and to get warmed up. Make sure everyone can hear everyone else and that you can clearly hear what you are doing. Don't go silly loud, you need to hear everything clearly. You can't turn the drums up (Unless your using an electric Kit), so if you can't hear the drums, then you are too loud!

If you are in a loud rock band, then make sure you are wearing ear plugs. You can buy ear plugs that are especially made for musicians, they kind of just turn the volume down a bit without ruining the sound.

Neither me, Kevin or Jamie wore ear plugs for the first few years, now we all have tinnitus! So we do now, and we all wish we had been wearing them from the start!

So now you've got your levels right and you're warmed up, what are you going to play?

I would suggest playing some covers to start with, learn a handful of tunes that you all like and just rock out. Have fun, play the covers in different styles, be silly, and just get used to how each of you play.

In Cujo we booked a rehearsal room from 7pm till 11pm every Thursday night for 10 years. We played together so often we were extremely tight. We could sense when one of us was going to break a song down or go crazy all out thrash, and we'd all follow in sync, solid as a rock! We were so tight and well-rehearsed that even though our style may not have been to everyone's taste, we always amazed audiences when we played on stage. People often said they couldn't believe the sound we produced as a three piece because it sounded like there were more instruments playing! I couldn't tell you exactly how we produced that sound, but we developed it over many hours of mucking around in the rehearsal studio developing our sound.

Record everything! You will probably jam over new songs loads of times before you are happy with them and during that time you might play something, possibly by accident, which sounded really cool. But chances are, especially if you did it by accident, you won't remember what you did. Being able to listen back to a rehearsal and remember all the bits that sounded great really help in producing great songs.

You might be at the stage where you have ten or so finished tracks and you've got a gig coming up, or you're about to go to a recording studio to record. If you've recorded that set in the rehearsal room, then you can listen back to it to make sure all the tunes are sounding great, none of you are making any mistakes, and the order you are playing them works well.

In Cujo we recorded every rehearsal. For the first few years we used a portable cassette player. We played so loud in the rehearsal room that we had to put the stereo in a room next door. The recordings weren't brilliant but it was enough to hear everything we had played. After a couple of years we upgraded to a little minidisc player with a condenser mic plugged in. This was much better, we could have the minidisc player in the room with us and we could also upload the rehearsal onto a computer and email it to each other as mp3's.

These days there are lots of different things you can record with: minidisk players, mp3 recorders, portable 4-tracks, laptops or probably even an app on your smart phone.

Not only do you get to hear back how the songs sounded, you can also use these recording to rehearse at home between rehearsals in the studio. Practice makes perfect! If you arrive at a rehearsal and you've not been practicing and everyone else has, they aren't going to be very happy with you!

When you rehearse for a gig, especially your first one, it's a good idea to play through your entire set a few times, in the order you plan to play it at the gig. Also, when you are in the rehearsal room practicing, you will all be facing each other. When you play a gig, you will be facing the audience. So try setting up the rehearsal room up like you are on stage at a gig facing an audience and make sure you can all play everything without having to see what each other are doing.

Time how long your set is. When you get gig bookings you will be given a certain amount of time on stage, typically 30 to 45 minutes, so it's important to work out a set that is the correct length. Also, time all your songs individually and note it down. If you know how long each song is, it's easier to play around with your set.

When putting a set together, It's a good idea to have a spare song. If you play your set too fast, instead of finishing early, you can play your spare song. Or, if you play an awesome gig and the audience want an encore, then you have an extra song to play.

Rehearsing tips:

- Arrive on time and set up quickly.
- Always take a notepad and note down everything you play so not to forget anything.
- Record everything!
- Guitarists take spare strings, plectrums and leads, drummers take spare skins.
- Wear ear plugs!
- Try rehearsing facing away from each other.
- Make friends with the people who run the rehearsal room, you never know when they might come in handy, or might help you become successful.
- Respect their equipment.
- Make sure all sound proof doors are closed.
- Take some refreshments.
- If it is an important rehearsal, make a schedule to make sure you run through everything you need to.
- Have fun!

WRITE IT

WRITING SONGS

There is no right or wrong way to write a song, all artists and bands do things differently; some people write the lyrics first; some write the lyrics last. Some people work out music by playing around on an instrument, some people think of a melody in their head! It doesn't matter where it comes from, and you will probably find all the songs you write originate in different ways.

Another way to think of a melody is in your sleep! Paul McCartney of the Beatles wrote Yesterday in his sleep! He woke up one morning with the complete melody in his head, he quickly wrote some lyrics to go with the melody so he didn't forget it. The original lyrics were "Scrambled eggs, Oh you've got such lovely legs, Scrambled eggs. Oh, my baby, how I love your legs."!

You will probably discover one or two of you in the band are better at coming up with the original idea for a song. It doesn't really matter where the idea came from, as long as everyone has an input in creating the song and you end up with a great sounding tune.

It's important everyone in your band gets involved with the writing process and you try out everyone's ideas. Every member will come up with ideas that the others won't have thought of, and it's all these different ideas that come together to create your bands identity - your original sound. Also, you don't want anyone to feel left out and feel that they aren't as important as the rest of the band.

In Cujo, most of our songs Kevin came up with the original idea, he would work something out on his guitar at home, probably a few chords and a melody and a handful of lyrics. He'd often record himself singing and playing the ideas on his acoustic guitar, then email them to us to listen to, so we could have a think about what we would play and have a practice before our next rehearsal. Or he'd just turn up to rehearsal with an idea, tell me the chords and we would all jam around that idea and see if a good tune developed from it. Sometimes it was me or Jamie came up with a song idea or a cool riff, or a song originated from a random jam.

So once you have got a great idea for a song, perhaps an amazing chorus and a couple of verses, how do you turn that into a finished song?

You need to work out a structure. Most pop songs follow a similar structure: Intro, Verse, Verse, Chorus, Verse, Chorus, outro; with perhaps a bridge or solo thrown in there somewhere.

You don't have to follow this structure, but you will find this structure does work well for most songs. You should structure it however it feels best. Your lyrics will tell some kind of story, so the music underneath it should suit the mood of the lyrics. If you think a particular song should have a quiet intro, quiet verse, and then a quiet instrumental that builds up and up to a massive loud chorus at the end, then do it. Write whatever you feel it should be, it's your song.

All verses in a song tend to be quite similar, the same with the choruses, but try to make some subtle changes to make the song more interesting, especially in the verses. Try different things out; maybe try a slightly different guitar riff, or bass line, or drum beat, or maybe break down one verse to just drums, bass and vocals, or just guitar and vocals. Have a listen to some of your favorite songs, listen for differences in the verses and choruses, you'll probably notice things you hadn't heard before.

You don't all need to be playing your instruments all the time, sometimes less is more. You want to send the listener on a journey, not only with the lyrics but the music as well. While you are working on a song, try cutting things out, for example; If you have a chorus you want to sound really loud and big when it comes in, then try cutting out some of the sound in the verse before it, so there is more of an impact when the chorus starts.

Drummers and bassists should really concentrate on what each other are doing. The bass should have a groove that follows what the drummer is doing with the bass drum. The drums and bass are the backbone to a song and they need to have a great groove going on between them.

Don't forget backing vocals, they can really change the sound of a song and give it more depth. They don't have to be much, just a simple harmony above or below what the lead vocal is doing can make a big difference. They don't have to be that loud or prominent either. I bet if you have a listen to your favorite album and really concentrate on listening to the vocals, you are likely to hear some backing vocals you never knew were there. And if they weren't there, it would sound quite different and probably not as good.

Remember to write a cool outro, this often gets forgotten. The outro is the last part of the song. You might have an amazing song, but if the last thing your audience hears is an awful ending, then that's what they are going to remember, so make sure the outro is good, and try make all your songs finish differently.

It's good to have a mixture of songs, as long as they are in a similar style. You can make some heavier, some more melodic, some upbeat, some sad, etc. If all your songs sound very similar, listening to your album or watching you play live will get a little boring for the audience. Also, if you tend to play a lot of heavy, loud songs, then a couple of quieter or slower ones in your live set is always a good idea. This will make it more interesting to the audience but will also give you a bit of a rest. Let the drummer rest his limbs for a few minutes, or the singer rest his voice. Gigs can be quite demanding on your body, so if you've just rocked out three or four ear-shattering songs, a few minutes of quiet is a welcome break.

Finishing songs can sometimes be difficult. You might start and finish writing a whole song over the course of one rehearsal, then some songs might take weeks or even months to finish.

If you get stuck trying to finish a song it can get quite frustrating. Maybe you have an amazing verse with a brilliant groove, but you just can't get the chorus to sound right, or you just can't work out how you get from a chorus back into verse. If you start to struggle it's usually a good idea to pause the writing of that song for a bit, move onto something else and come back to it later or another day. Listening to the same bit of a song over and over again can just fry your brain. You will probably come up with a whole load of new ideas once you've stopped thinking about that song for a bit.

Another thing to bear in mind is song length. Pop songs tend to be around three to three and a half minutes. One of the main reasons for this, is because radio stations tend to only play songs for about three minutes. If you have a song you think would do well on a commercial radio station, then make it around three minutes long. Don't let the three minute thing bog you down though, you don't have to make them radio friendly, they should be as long as you feel they should be.

In Cujo our shortest song was called 'Forty five'. We called it forty five because once we had recorded the song the producer said, "That was only forty five seconds long!" So that's what we called it! We had another song that went on for nearly ten minutes. If we had tried to make either of those songs three minute long, they just wouldn't have been as good.

As I mentioned earlier in the book, when you are writing songs, or just jamming, make sure you record everything! It's very easy to forget things you have just made up. You will be gutted if you wrote something really cool and can't remember what it was!

When we were writing songs in Cujo, I often had trouble thinking of a cool bass line to fit with a new song whilst we were in rehearsals. Being able to take a recording away with me was really handy. Sometimes I got Jamie and Kevin to play through a new song and record it without me playing any bass, then I would have all week to listen to it and play along to it at home. I would also listen to it in the car on my way to and from work and think of the bass lines in my head. Then I would work out on my bass what I had in my head. Having a recording also meant Kevin and Jamie didn't have to keep playing the same thing over and over again until I figured something cool out!

If you decide you want to write a whole album. Make sure you write more songs than you need. You can then choose the best ones for your album. If you plan to have ten songs on your album, then write fifteen.

In Cujo, every time we had about fifteen new songs, we would decide to record a new album. We would listen to all the recordings we'd done in rehearsals and decide, out of those fifteen songs which ten were the best. We would then go and record those ten songs. Once recorded we would listen to the new recordings and decide which ones would make it onto the album. Sometimes we decided that only seven or eight of them where good enough.

So when you are writing your songs, try and remember all the tips I've highlighted in this chapter, but the most important thing to do is just keep writing. The more you write, the better you get.

WRITING LYRICS

Before you can start writing any lyrics, you need some inspiration. Inspiration can come from anywhere, maybe something that's happened to you in your life, or an idea from another song or poem, or from a newspaper or magazine article, or maybe even a Facebook post. It doesn't really matter where you get the idea from, as long as it means something to you. It's easier if the subject has some similarities to something you have experienced in the past, something that brings up some emotions.

Like writing the music, writing lyrics can be done in many different ways, and no way is right or wrong, but it is usually easier to start by writing the chorus

Perhaps you've decided what you want to write a song from inspiration you found in a newspaper headline. Try writing the chorus, maybe that headline could be the lyrics in the chorus. Every chorus in a song is usually the same, or very similar, so once you've figured out what the lyrics are for the chorus then you can leave that and start working on the verses.

The verses are the main bulk of a song, verses will have a lot more lines than the chorus and tell the story behind the chorus.

Think about the song structure, how do you want this song to sound, how many verses and choruses, are you going to have a bridge or middle eight, do they have words in?

The bridge is a short section used to bridge the gap between a verse and a chorus. It could be two or four bars long and it's often used when the verse and chorus are so different from each other that a 'joining' phrase helps bring them together."

A middle eight is the same as a bridge except it is eight or more bars long. Some people think it is an alternative verse, with different chords to the verse, which is one way you can look at it. If a song has a middle-eight it will typically be in the second half of the song.

Try using different perspectives. For example, you could describe an event in the first verse, and add perspective by describing how it affected you or made you feel in the second verse. Another viewpoint can put an interesting spin on it.

Try to avoid writing obvious things, for example, don't write 'I'm feeling really sad', try and describe the fact that you are feeling sad in other words; what it feels like to be that sad or how it has changed your life.

You don't need to make everything rhyme. You are limited to what words rhyme with each other, so if you try and make everything rhyme, you could end up with some really cheesy lyrics, or lyrics that don't really make sense.

Try being clever with your rhymes, you don't want to just use a load of hard rhymes like Love and Dove, or Say and Day. You can use longer words where just part of the word rhythms, or try using slant rhythms. Slant rhythms are two words that share a final consonant sound or a final vowel sound, but not both. For example, the following are slant rhythms "soul" and "all", or "on" and "moon".

Some people can think of lyrics really quickly. For me, it takes ages! I like to use the notepad app on my phone; every time I have an idea for a song, I write it down. If I overhear someone say something, or read something interesting and a few song lyrics popped into my head, I write it down.

When I am trying to write a song, and I run out of ideas, I have a look through all the notes on my phone. I also try and write quickly and write a lot more lyrics than I need, then I go back through it and whittle it down.

Apparently Mark Knopfler wrote the Dire Straits song Money for Nothing after overhearing delivery men in a New York department store complain about their jobs while watching

MTV. He wrote the song in the store sitting at a kitchen display they had set up. Many of the lyrics were things they actually said.

I have a couple of other apps I use regularly when writing. One is a thesaurus app, which helps you find alternative words. This is great if you have something you want to write, but the line doesn't fit because one of the words has too many or too little syllables in. I would put that word into the thesaurus and find other words that mean the same thing. Hopefully I find a good word with the right amount of syllables, or a new way to describe what I am trying to say.

The other app is a rhyming app. You put in a word and it gives you all the different words that rhyme with it. If you are like me and failed your English GCSE 3 times, then apps like this to help you write are really handy!

If you start getting frustrated because you can't think of anything decent to write; stop writing and leave it for a few hours, or till another day. It helps to rest your brain for a bit, then come back to it later, as you will probably have a load of new ideas.

If you're not a naturally good writer, it doesn't mean you can't write great lyrics, you just need to practice. Don't be disheartened if your lyrics aren't perfect on the first draft. Many professional writers will rewrite a song's lyrics dozens of times before they make it onto a record.

RECORDING

So what do you need to record a single, EP or album? Aside from a band and a load of great songs, you need a recording studio and a producer.

Recording studios will have everything you need to record your music, apart from instruments, and maybe instrument amps. They may have instrument amps which you are able to use, but if you want to achieve the exact sound you normally get, then it's best to take your own amps. The Producer might suggest using one of their amps, if they think it will sound better.

Recording studios are usually made up of a few different rooms; probably a big band room like a rehearsal studio, and then a control room where the producer sits with the mixing desk and all the other recording equipment, then some smaller rooms which might be a drum room and a vocal room/booth.

Large recording studios might have many rooms and will have a number of staff working there, but the kind of studio you will be recording in will probably just have one person, the Producer.

The Producer is a recording and sound engineer who knows how to do the whole process; from setting up all the instruments, amps and microphones, to recording, mixing and mastering.

It is important to choose the right producer for your music. You need to be confident with the producer you choose, so you can allow them to work their magic to get the most out of your recording!

Maybe you already have a studio in mind, or you have been recommended a good one. If not, have a look online at the studios in your area. Any decent studio will have a website with all the info you need to know about the studio: the facilities, the equipment they use, their producers and also some of the bands they have produced.

You might not know what all the equipment is that they boast about having, but it doesn't really matter what equipment they use, as long as they get good results.

You've probably put a lot of time and effort in to writing these songs, so you want to find the best studio and the best producer you can for your budget.

If the producer doesn't have any examples of the music they have produced on their website, then email them and ask where you can have a listen; if it sounds really good and the kind of recording you are looking for, then give them a call to discuss your requirement and costs.

The studio will want to know: how many people are in your band, what instruments you will be recording, what style of recording you are looking for and how many songs you would like to record. If the discussion goes well and you are happy with the price they quote, and the producer sounds confident that he can produce the kind of recording you are looking for, then work out some dates and get it booked in.

In Cujo we rehearsed every week in a studio owned by Brian Nash, the guitarist and songwriter from famous 1980's pop band Frankie Goes to Hollywood. Brian would often pop into our rehearsals and help us out with our song writing. When we were ready to record our second album, Brian recommended a producer he knew called Tim Hamill, who owned a studio called Sonic One in Llanelli in Wales. We got in touch with Tim and he sent us some samples of other bands he had produced. The music he sent us sounded awesome, and because he was a mate of Brian, he gave us a really good price. We booked two days with Tim, booked a few days off work, booked our train tickets and a hotel in Llanelli and off we went!

Away from the hustle and bustle of London, out in the countryside away from any distractions, it was a great experience. Tim was a really nice guy, he was into the same kind of music as us and loved our tracks and had loads of experience producing similar music.

Once you have identified the studio/producer that is right for you, you need to decide with the producer how you want to do your recording.

Recording a song, EP or Album doesn't have to cost that much and doesn't have to take very long at all. You hear stories of bands taking years and spending thousands recording an album. You also hear stories od bands like 'The Animals' recording 'House of the Rising Sun', live in one take in fifteen minutes! And that song sounds great!

The first time we recorded in Cujo, we didn't really know what we were doing, we didn't have any experience recording. The producer wasn't very experienced either, so we did what we thought we were supposed to do which was to record everything separately. We recorded the drums, then the bass, then the guitars then the vocals.

After recording we sat with the sound engineer mixing the tracks. Once we heard everything put together we realised that it didn't really sound like us. We had all held back in our performances. We hadn't been playing or singing like we normally did live or in rehearsals. This was because we had all played a lot softer than usual, partly because we were nervous about making a mistake but also because we all felt a bit embarrassed playing solo and rocking out in front of everyone.

The first time you record you will probably feel like this too. Try and forget that everyone is around you listening to what you are playing, and just relax, get into the groove, rock out and play the song as you would in rehearsals.

When we recorded that second album down in Wales with Tim, we wanted to make sure we got the live energetic rock sound we always got live. So we decided to record everything completely live.

It took two days to produce ten songs. On the first day we recorded ten tracks, the second day Tim mixed and mastered them all. This worked perfectly, the recordings came out exactly how we sounded in the rehearsal room with all the raw grungyness we wanted. We left with an awesome sounding album. A whole album, recorded, mixed and mastered in 2 days!

If you are going to record live you need to make sure you all know exactly what you are going to play and that you can play all the tracks without making mistakes. When recording live like this, all the microphones will pick up all the other sounds. So if someone accidently sung the wrong lyric, you can't just re-record that vocal track as that vocal would have been picked up on other microphones, you would have to start the recording from scratch.

Out of the ten songs we recorded on that album with Tim, some songs we did in one take, some took three or four attempts, but at the end of the day we had recorded ten songs. This also made it quite quick and easy for the sound engineer to mix and master.

On day two we sat around drinking a few beers watching the engineer do his stuff. By the end of day two we left the recording studio with a CD with ten great sounding songs that were a good enough standard to be played on any radio station (and some of them were) and an album we were really proud of. We couldn't wait to play it to our friends and family and excited about the reaction we would get from the music industry when we started posting them out.

We recoded two more albums in that live way and they all sounded great. Our fifth album we wanted a similar live sound but wanted it to sound a bit more polished. So we went about that recording slightly differently. We recorded each song initially like we did before, all playing at the same time like we did on the previous album, but then we recorded everything again. Jamie went into a drum booth and played the drums again whist in his headphones listening to the songs we'd just recorded, minus the drums. I did the same with the bass, Kevin did his guitars again, and then we did all the vocals again. We recorded everything separately but we were all listening to the recording we did live so we had that live feeling when we were playing, which came out in the recording.

As everything was recorded separately, the engineer had better control of each recorded instrument to move volume levels up and down, fix any dud notes and add effects. We ended up with a much more polished finished product.

Once you have chosen which songs you will record, how you will record them and you have booked your recording sessions, all you need to do now is practice. Make sure you all know the songs like the back of your hands. You don't want to be wasting time on the day working bits out or replaying parts you have played wrong.

When the day comes and you arrive at the studio, the producer will tell you where to set up. Depending on how you have decided to record, the amps may be in different rooms to where you are playing, there might be a drum booth and separate vocal booths. If you are recording live, then you might just be set up in the one room as you do in rehearsals. The producer will then plug everything in; microphones will be set up in front of your amps, all around the drum kit and be plugged directly into to mixing desk in the control room. You might not be playing out loud like in rehearsals, you may all be given headphones so you can hear yourself, and the rest of the band play.

The reason you wear headphones is to avoid sound leaking onto other microphones. For example, the person singing the vocals will be in a soundproof vocal booth and can hear all the music in the headphones, so when they sing all the microphone will pick up is the vocals. The producer will then have a clean vocal track to play with. If the vocal track had also picked up all the other sounds, and the producer wanted to turn up or down that vocal in a mix or perhaps wanted to add some effects to the vocal; they couldn't because any change they make would also change the sound of everything else the microphone picked up.

Once everything is set up, you will sound check all the instruments. The producer will ask one of you at a time to play your instrument so he can listen and check the signal is good. They will need a clear recording of everything with no buzzing or interference.

If you do get buzzing from your guitar, there is a little trick you can do to stop it. The buzzing means your guitar isn't properly earthed. At some point you will need to check the guitars wiring but for now, grab a spare guitar string, tie it to something metal on your guitar, then run the rest of the string down your trouser leg.- buzzing gone!

Everything must be perfectly in tune, so make sure you take your tuners with you. You will need to check your tuning after everything you play.

The producer will tell you when to start playing. If something isn't right, of if someone makes a mistake, the producer will tell you to stop playing and start that part again. This can get frustrating if it keeps happening. However, don't get annoyed with the producer, they will be a lot more experienced than you, and know what they are talking about. If your timings keep speeding up or slowing during a song, they might suggest you play along to a click track.

Once you have recorded your tracks, your job is pretty much done, the producer will now mix them. They will have already done a rough mix whilst you are recording.

Mixing is when the producer puts all the tracks together, and makes sure everything is in time and at the right volume levels and adds various compressors and effects. Whilst mixing the producer might suggest things like cutting certain bits out, or double tracking a guitar to give a bigger sound. It's worth trying out whatever they suggest, but don't be scared to say if you don't like something, it's your recording and you're probably paying quite a lot of money for this, so it's important it sounds exactly how you want it.

Usually once the tracks are all mixed, the producer will give you a copy of all the tracks on a CD to go away and listen to for a few days. This is a good idea as your brain will be tired of hearing the same songs being played over and over again. Give your ears a rest and listen again the next day. Listen to what it sounds like on different systems: on your home stereo, in your car, through headphones, etc. You want it to sound good wherever people listen to it.

You might want a few changes, maybe the volumes need altering a bit to make one of the instruments stand out a bit more. Give your requests to the producer to do the final mix.

After the producer has done the final mix, the tracks will then be mastered. Some producers might send them off to a professional mastering engineer to do this or some can do it themselves.

I don't really know everything that is involved in mastering, not all producers can do it well. It's a bit of an art apparently.

Mastering will kind of polish the sound of your album by changing the EQ, gain, and compression to give it a consistent sound from track to track. This process also allows them to pump up the volume of your overall album so it's as loud as can be. It will sound better than the final mix did. You probably won't be able to hear what is different, it will just sound more awesome than it did already!

Once mastered, you have your final product! The Producer will give you a master CD. The tracks on the master CD will be saved as very high quality files. Don't lose that CD, you will need it to make copies and to get your CD's produced.

HOME RECORDING

A very cost effective way to record is to record your album in a home studio. Though you will never be able to produce something as good as a proper studio recording, you can get pretty close to it if you know what you are doing.

These days a lot of people learn music production skills at school and college. If you have these skills then you can probably put together a pretty good sounding demo, or even a professional sounding album.

Most people wouldn't be able to set up and play a drum kit in their house, not without the neighbors calling the police! Unless you are going for an electric drum sound and can get away with programming the drums you might have to record the drums in a studio then record everything else from home.

The two most popular professional recording programs are Cubase and Logic. I don't really know if one is better than the other, everyone has their own preference. People who have an apple computer typically use Logic and people who have a windows PC's use Cubase.

I use Cubase at home. I only know how to use about 20% of the software but that's enough to produce some great sounding music.

I'm not going to teach you how to record your own stuff at home, that would fill an entire book! It's a great skill to learn and a lot of fun. You could buy some recording software and teach yourself from the manual or by watching YouTube tutorials, but there are also a lot of good college courses out there too.

DESIGNING YOUR ALBUM

Once you have recorded your album you need to decide on an album title, which songs make it onto the album, in which order, and the artwork for the cover. If you are producing CD's you will also need to design the CD spine, the back cover and the insides.

Title

Your album title needs to reflect what the album is about and needs to fit your bands image. Often bands us their band name as the title for their first album, or they use one of the song titles as the album name - usually the song they plan to release first. These are both good ideas, but it can be anything you want. Try and choose something that your fans can relate to.

Use your fans. Ask all your friends and followers on social

media to suggest names for the title, maybe even offer a prize for the person who comes up with the best name. Involving your fans in anything is always a good idea, plus they will give loads of different ideas that you would never have thought of.

Once you do have some good ideas for the title, check on-line to make sure they aren't already being used by another band, you don't really want to use the same album title as another band!

Tracks

Which songs should you put on the album?

There isn't really a rule on how many songs there should be on an album, but record companies tend to recommend that the album should be about 40 minutes long, spread out over about 10 songs. But you could have anything between 5 and 30!

An EP (stands for Extended Play) is more music than a single, but too short to qualify as a full album. If you do only have a few songs, then putting out an EP is probably a better idea.

You want the album to be a collection of your best songs, and you want them all to relate to each other somehow. Don't put half decent – album filler tracks on to bulk it out. If you have recorded twelve songs, but two of them aren't as good as the rest then only put the ten good ones on.

Choosing which songs should go on your album can be

difficult. As you wrote and recorded the songs, they probably all sound great to you, and all your band members might have a different view on which ones are best.

Who is going to buy this album? Your fans. So who should you ask? Your fans!

When we released our last Cujo album, we wanted to release one of the tracks first as a single, but we couldn't decide which track it should be. We had narrowed it down to our two favorites. So for a limited time of two weeks we put all our new album tracks up on our Myspace page and asked all our followers to vote for their favorite song. Loads of people voted which was great and what was interesting was, they didn't pick either of the ones we thought they would like, the majority of them picked a completely different one! We released that song and it was a success! It almost made the UK charts!

So ask your fans, they will always be happy to help.

Song order

If your songs play out a story, then you already have an obvious order, but make sure the first song is one of the best on the album. Don't put similar sounding songs together and spread the possible singles out over the album.

Since music streaming services started a few years ago, recent studies suggest that songs at the start of an album are more likely to be streamed more than the ones at the end. With this in mind, you should put what you think are the best songs on the first half of the album.

Artwork

Your album, EP or Single cover is an important image. It is the first thing people are going to see before they hear your music, so it needs to be a striking image that will make people interested in hearing your music.

The cover needs to represent your band, your style of music and the songs or story of your album. Using an image of someone's face is a popular theme, and a design that works very well. Whatever you decide, make sure it's quite a simple and bold image.

Be careful not to just use an image you have found on the internet, without checking if you can use it or not. You have three options: you can use one of your own photos or designs, you can search for royalty free images on the internet, or you can buy a stock photo. Websites like Shutterstock or 123RF have thousands of great images which won't cost very much to buy and use.

Remember this image is often going to be seen very small, thumbnail size on places like iTunes and Soundcloud, and in website and magazine reviews. When you have found an image, shrink it down to thumbnail size to see what it looks like; does it still look good or is the image too small to be seen clearly? It will also need to be enlarged for flyers and posters so make sure the image you have is a very good quality.

CD's are square, so your image needs to be square. CD covers are roughly five by five inches, or twelve by twelve centimeters.

If you are going to get CD's printed then there are a few other parts that you will need to design as well: the back cover, the inner sleeve, the spine, and the CD itself. There are loads of templates online that you can download to help you. If you are going to get a company to burn your CD's and print your CD artwork, then they will typically have their own templates that they will send you.

You don't necessarily have to put your band name on the album cover, or even the album name. Everywhere your album will be online will have your band name and album title next to it in text, so it doesn't need to be on the cover. Whatever you decide, make sure your band name and album title are written clearly on the spine of your CD's.

We will look at CD production in more detail later in this book when we get into releasing music. However, you might just want to produce a handful of CD demo's to help you get gigs booked, give out to family and friends or to sell at local gigs. Rather than using a company to produce your CDs you can burn some on your own PC. Most PC's will have some kind of CD burning software on them which usually provide templates for printing your own sleeve. You can buy packs of blank CDs and cases at most supermarkets, and also you can buy printer paper with CD shaped stickers on that you can print onto and stick on the CD's. So you can easily knock up 20 or 30 CD's at home. I wouldn't recommend selling these online or sending out to radio stations, unless they look really good, you really want good quality professionally produced CD's for that.

GIG IT

GIGGING

Probably the best part of being in a band is playing live, especially in a big venue with hundreds of fans dancing, moshing, stage diving and singing your lyrics back at you.

In this chapter we will be talking about how to book, prepare for, and play gigs.

Before you can play the big venues you will need to have built up a good following. The larger the following you have, the larger the venues you will be booked at. You have to start small and build your audience.

If you haven't done any gigs yet, you want to start gigging as local as possible; venues that are easy for your friends and family to get to without having to drive far. You will have a better chance of attracting more people locally, and these gigs will be good practice for playing larger more important gigs. You will also earn some cash to put towards rehearsals and recordings.

You don't want to play too often in the same area, If you do then you won't get as many people along. So leave about six to eight weeks between gigs in the same area.

Jamie, Kevin and I lived in Enfield, so we started off playing at a few pubs around Enfield, quite often with another local band called The Tide, who were old school mates of ours. Between the two bands we had lots of family and friends, so our gigs were always packed with a hundred plus people. Because the gigs were always packed, this attracted lots of new local people who we didn't know, and often the local newspapers.

Once we had built up a good following in Enfield, we started playing further afield. Fortunately for us, Enfield is in North London, a few miles from Camden Town where there are tons of well-known venues. So we started playing regular gigs at venues in and around Camden like the Dublin Castle, The Bull & Gate, The Hope & Anchor and The Purple Turtle; building up a large and loyal fan base. It was harder to get people to travel into Camden from Enfield so we started off with only about twenty people attending, but over time we started to attract up to a hundred people. This enabled us to start playing larger, better known venues like The Barfly, The Astoria, The Garage and The Underworld. We then started to attract between two to three hundred people. This then enabled us to get slots at big festivals and support slots with well-known bands.

Find out which venues have live band nights in your area. These venues are likely to be pubs, social clubs and sports clubs. (I'm going to refer to all these smaller gigs as pubs gigs).

Pubs don't tend to do things by email, and phone calls can be difficult so the best thing to do is go down there during the daytime, when it's quiet and have a chat to the manager or landlord. They might want to listen to a demo of your band, and they will want to know how many people you expect to attend. The more people who come along, the more money they make on the bar. The more money they make on the bar, the more they can pay you, and the more likely you are to be invited back to play again.

There are four main types of pub gigs.

1: Paid cover gigs.

This is when the pub hire a band to entertain their customers. You will need to play well known songs that everyone will know (you can usually slip one or two of your own in). You will probably be paid somewhere between £50 and £200. You may or may not be expected to bring and audience.

These gigs aren't great for getting your own songs heard but they do give you good experience at playing live and playing lots of other bands material, which will give you some good ideas when you write your own songs, and you earn you some cash to put towards the band costs. It will also help you build your fan base and mailing list.

2: Band nights.

These gigs you can play your own songs. Some venues will put on two or three bands in one evening. They are great for getting your songs heard by new people because you will be playing to your own fans but also the fans of the other bands.

You will usually be paid based on how many people you bring along to the gig. It may be something like: £5 per person to get in and you get £1.50 of that. So if twenty people come to see your band, you get £30. So not a huge amount of money, but these gigs are all about getting your music out there and building up your fan base, rather than making money.

3: Battle of the Bands.

Quite a few pubs hold band competitions. They usually hold different heats over a number of weeks, probably three bands per night, then a final at the end with one band crowned the winner. You don't always get paid anything for these gigs and some even charge to enter, so sometimes they can be a bit of a con. Quite often the winner of each heat is the band who brings the most people (the band who makes the pub the most money). Unfortunately, these events can sometimes be all about making money for the pub and don't do a lot to help the band. However, there are some good ones out there; some you get paid for, some with music industry judges, and some with really great prizes. If there is a battle of the bands competition near you, find out a bit about it before you enter and decide if you think it's worth it or not.

We entered a few in Cujo and we weren't particularly impressed with any of them.

One Battle of the Bands competition we entered, we weren't getting paid for, but we were told there were going to be loads of music industry people attending and judging. We were headlining the night so we were first to sound check. After our sound check we watched the organisers collecting loads of money from the other four bands who were also performing that night. We then had a chat with the organisers and realised they weren't very nice people and they didn't really have anyone very important coming from the music industry like they had advertised, it was all a bit of a con. We were so annoyed, we secretly sneaked our equipment out the back and left. I would have loved to be a fly on the wall when they announced their headline band and no-one came out!

During another Battle of the bands competition, we got through to the final. This competition was judged on how many people came to see you. So when we discovered we were in the final against a band from the University round the corner, (who had 10 people in their band, and had brought all their families and all the students from the campus next door) we knew we didn't stand a chance of winning, there were hundreds of them!

Even though we had quite a few fans attending, and our mates found out where the venue kept the voting slips, (stole loads of them and filled them in) we still didn't have enough to win! However, we got to play to all these people who hadn't heard us before and we picked up a few new fans, so it was worth it.

4: Your own event.

You can put on your own events by hiring out part of a pub or function room/hall. You might have to pay to use this room, or you might not. If you guarantee the pub that you will be bringing a large audience, they may give you the room for free because they know they will make a lot of money behind the bar.

You can make good money from these gigs and there are a few different ways you can do this, depending on what the pub are happy to do.

You could run the door yourselves, sell tickets prior to the gig and on the door and make all that money yourself; Or the pub may run the door, charge people entry but give you a percentage of the ticket price; Or the pub may pay you a fee depending on how much money they take behind the bar during the gig.

For these gigs you will probably have to do everything yourself: set up the room, set up the stage, set up all the equipment, run the door and clean up after; so you will probably need some help from friends.

As it's your own event you can play whatever you want, maybe play all your own songs but add a few covers. If there are a load of people there who don't know your songs, playing a few covers that they do know will help to get them up dancing and have a good time. You can play covers in your own style and make them your own.

Invite another one or two bands as support acts, this will help to get a bigger crowd along, ultimately get more fans and make more money.

Pub gigs can be great fun but can be stressful getting everything set up. Unlike music venues, pubs don't tend to have their own PA system or a sound engineer. This is something you will have to sort out yourself. If you don't own a PA system, you will have to hire one. You will have to set it all up and sound check yourselves, which can be quite difficult if you've not done it before.

There are lots of companies online who rent our PA systems for gigs, hopefully you can find one local to you. Give them a call and see what they offer. Some companies will drop the system off and collect it; some will set it up for you, and some even provide a sound engineer. The most cost effective option is to pick it up, set it all up yourself, and drop it back the next day.

Tell the PA hire company the size of the room you are playing in and the line-up of your band, and they will work out the size/wattage of the PA amp you need.

If the room in the pub you are playing in is quite small, then you might only need a PA for the vocals. So let's say you have: two singers; a lead vocals and a backing singer. The size of PA you need would be something like 100 watts, probably with four inputs and a couple of speakers. This arrangement is quite easy to set up yourself and get the volume levels right during sound check.

If the room is quite big, like a big hall or function room, then you might want to mic up all the instruments. If so, you will need a louder PA, maybe 500W or 1000W, with ten or so inputs, 2 - 4 speakers and stands, 2 bass speakers (aka bass bins), and the various different vocal, instrument and drum microphones and stands. If you need a PA this size, then you probably need a sound engineer, as setting up and sound checking is not a simple task and takes some time.

Alternatively you can buy your own PA system. You can pick up a decent second-hand one for around two to three hundred pounds. You'll have to work out how to set it up but a good investment if you're able to store one and transport to gigs.

If you are doing the sound yourself, once you have set up and got the volume levels roughly right, then get someone to stand at the back of the room and make sure they can hear everything. The sound can be quite different once the room is full of people so you will need someone to do the same once you've started playing the gig and throughout, keeping you informed so you can turn things up or down when required.

Quite a lot of pubs have a noise limiters. Noise limiters detect the volume levels and cut the electricity to the plug sockets around the stage if the noise reaches a certain level. Often these noise level detectors are enforced upon the pub by the local council because of neighboring properties complaining about the noise. With this in mind, make sure you ask the pub if they have a noise limiter, and if so, test your levels during sound check to make sure you don't cut the sound. You don't want this to happen half way through a song!

Cujo were a very loud band so we always set these things off! Some of the pubs we played in let us run an extension lead from the stage to the bar or elsewhere in the pub so when the noise limiter cut the power to the stage, we weren't using those plugs, so it didn't cut our power!

Pubs don't tend to have good lighting for gigs, so check out what the lighting is like before your gig. PA hire companies often provide lighting rig hire too, so this is something you could consider. Having great lighting makes a big difference to gig.

In Cujo we knew a great local sound engineer called Vince Cooper. Vince would deliver his PA system, speakers, microphones, stands, lighting rig, etc. set it all up, sound check us, engineer the gig, then pack it up at the end and take it away. We normally paid about £150 for this. Sometimes he wouldn't be available himself so we would collect his PA and do it all ourselves. This was quite difficult at first but once we'd done it a few times we knew what we were doing. So find yourself a Vince!

Music venue gigs

Once you've got a few local gigs under your belt and you've got a great sounding live set, then time to get some music venues bookings. Playing in a purpose built music venue is a lot simpler than putting on a gig yourself. Music venues have promoters, door staff, sound engineers, a stage, a permanent PA system, stage lighting, etc. Some even have house drum kits and instrument amps you can use.

Normally venues don't book their own acts, this is done by a promoter or promotion company. Promoters will typically book three bands a night: a headline band and two support bands.

Have a look online at the different venue's websites and have a look at their gig listings. They should list who is promoting each evening. If it's not on the website, you can call the venue to find out. You want to find promoters who put on nights with bands of a similar genre to you.

The promoter is going to want to speak to you on the phone and hear a demo of your music. They will need to know how many of you in the band, what the line-up is, where you're from, how experienced and successful you are, and how many fans generally attend your gigs.

A promoter isn't going to book you if he doesn't like your

demo, but he also won't book you if you if they think you're not going to bring an audience. Like the situation with the pubs, if a venue's promoter is booking bands who don't have a following, the venue won't make any money on the bar or door and likely to stop using that promoter.

When you start playing venues, you will get the support slots: first or second on stage. As you get better and more popular then they will promote you to headline slots.

Getting paid for these gigs is different to when you play pubs. Usually you will either have to sell tickets, or it's done on a flyer system. If it is the flyer system, when you are booking the gig the promoter will either give you a load of their flyers or give you all the details for you to produce your own. You need to find out your stage times, the entry price, the flyer discount price and what cut you get paid.

Every band on the bill will have their own flyers. When guests arrive at the venue, the person on the pay desk or box office desk will ask them which band they have come to see. At the end of the night, they will add up all the entry fees and pay you the agreed cut. So perhaps the entry fee is £10 and you get £3 of that. So if you get 30 people along, you get £60. This should be enough to cover your travel and a few drinks. But the idea isn't really to make money on these gigs - you are building you fan base and probably inviting music industry and media people along to perhaps review the gig.

You normally get a small guest list, maybe one person per band member. These people get in free of charge, so you won't get any cash for this. Unless you need to use it, probably best not to give them away. If you have invited music press or industry people along, they will expect to be on the guest list, so definitely use those free tickets for them. If you would like to add more people to the guest list, you can get more from the promoter, but you will have to pay for them.

Festivals

Once you're experienced playing small venues and you've built up a large following, then you want to start playing larger venues and festivals. These are also booked by promoters so you need to research who these people or companies are. It is unlikely that you will get booked just off the back of a good demo. You need to prove you are an upcoming band with a large following. Ideally by now you will have had some radio airplay and some good reviews in well-known publications. You will need a good press release to give them as well as your demo. I will be covering how to write a press release later in this book.

At festivals there are usually a lot more people involved in set up and engineering. There might be a stage manager, a couple of sound engineers, lighting engineers, roadies, etc. You might have a sound desk with an engineer to the side of the stage monitoring the stage sound and taking your requests for changes in monitor volumes, and a sound engineer on a desk out front monitoring and adjusting the sound that the audience hears.

There will probably be roadies that will help you get set up, and be around the stage to run on and assist if something has gone wrong, For example you might knock your microphone stand over, a roadie will run on and pick it up for you; or maybe you tread on your guitar lead and pull it out, they will run on stage and plug you back in.

Roadies are great. I remember the first gig Cujo did when we had roadies. We were playing a big gig for Pepe Jeans over in Madrid in Spain. They carried all our equipment for us and set it up. All I had to carry was my guitar! I walked on stage and a roadie ran over and plugged my guitar in and I was all ready to start playing. During the gig I knocked over my bottle of water, a roadie ran past, picked my bottle up and replaced it with a new one! It was awesome, I felt like a proper rock star!

Getting paid will be different again. Unless you're one of the bigger bands, who just get paid loads of money, you might have to sell some tickets. You will be given perhaps 50 tickets that you have to sell yourselves. You will have to pay the promoter for all 50 tickets so ideally you want to sell them all. You will probably get them at a discounted rate, so if you sell all your tickets you will make a little profit. You could sell them at the discounted price to your fans if you're not bothered in making a profit. If it is a particularly big gig which will give you some great exposure, then making a bit off a loss might be worth it.

For the festivals you might also receive a payment from PRS

(The Performing Rights Society). You won't know how much this payment will be until it lands in your bank account a few month after the festival. I will go into more detail about PRS later in this book; but for festivals, the organisers will pay a license fee to PRS, then a percentage of that fee is broken down and distributed to all the acts. Most of the money goes to the headline acts on the main stages. You will only get this payment if you are registered with PRS.

We played a few big festivals in Cujo, the biggest being the o2 Wireless Festival in Hyde Park. We received over £1000 for playing the Wireless Festival. At the time we didn't really know much about PRS but we were registered, and we certainly didn't know we were going to get paid anything. So we were very surprised when a few months after the festival, a payment of over a thousand pounds appeared in our bank account!

GIG PREPARATION AND SET-UP

When you play a venue, small or large, you will be given an arrival time, or load in time. Make sure you leave enough time to find the venue, load in and park your vehicle. Being late doesn't just piss off the promoters, it also stresses you out, which is the last thing you need especially if you are nervous about the gig.

When you arrive, go in and find out where to load in. They might have some back doors that you can load in rather than carry everything through the venue. When you load in, don't just put your gear on the stage, put it on the floor somewhere near the stage and wait for the Sound Engineer to instruct you.

Make an effort to get on with the engineer, introduce yourself, ask their name and find out a bit about them. Ask them how the evening is going to work and how they want to do everything.

Usually bands will sound check before the venue's music room is open to the public. The Headline band sound checks first, then the middle bands, then the first band. The last band to sound check, is first band on stage, so everything is already set up ready to go.

You may share equipment with other bands, maybe a bass amp or drum kit. This is so the changeover of bands is done as quickly as possible.

Some musicians don't like sharing their equipment, which is fine, but it makes things a lot easier if everyone is happy to share. It's much better if you can just walk on stage, plug in and play, rather than lugging your amps on and off stage whilst the audience is watching. You also feel a lot cooler, more like a big rock star, if you can just walk on, play a banging set, and then just walk off after!

When it's your turn to sound check, get set up quickly and wait for the engineers instructions. Don't mess around in the sound check and don't use it as a free rehearsal, you will just annoy the sound engineer, the other bands and waste time. The sound engineer has to get you set up and sound checked as quickly as possible. They are in full control of your sound throughout your gig, so if you have unintentionally pissed them off, they might not be too bothered about making sure you have a great sound.

Normally the drums will be set up and sound checked first, every different drum and cymbal will have its own little drum microphone. You start by checking the bass drum, when the engineer is happy with the sound, you move on to the floor tom, then rack toms, and so on until everything have been checked.

Whilst that is going on, everyone else in the band should be setting up their instruments and amps. Once the engineer is finished with the drums, you will move onto checking the instruments, one at a time, then the vocals. Following this you usually play one song, this gives the engineer a chance to set the levels and note them down for your set.

You will have a number of monitor speakers on the stage. These are speakers that are directed at you rather than at the audience, usually one for each band member. It's up to you what you choose to hear in your monitor speaker. The engineer will ask each of you what you want. You might want a mix of everything, or perhaps more of your own instrument. I usually play in loud rock bands, so I don't usually have any issues hearing what everyone else is playing, so I tend to have just my vocals in my monitor speaker.

Some gigs you don't get to do a full sound check, you just do what is called a line check. The sound engineer will just check the levels of everything, you don't play any songs and the first song you play will be the first song of your set. This is a lot quicker process and some venues do it this way.

Doing a line check rather than a full on Sound Check can be a bit daunting at first, as you don't know what it is all going to sound like when you start playing. You might start playing and you can't hear yourself, or something else you need to hear. If this is the case then you need to signal to the engineer after the first song to let him know what you need. Perhaps you need to hear more drums, so when you have the engineer's attention, then point at the drummer, then point in the air, this will tell the engineer that you want them to turn up the volume of the drums in your monitor. Or perhaps the guitarist is too loud (they usually are!), catch the attention of the engineer, point at the guitarist and then point down. He'll know that you are signaling to turn down the guitar in your monitor speaker.

Once you've done a few gigs like this, you get used to this, and you'll learn how to easily and discretely let the sound engineer know what you want whilst you're playing your set.

After all the sound checks are done, you then have to wait until it's your time to go on stage; this can sometimes be a long wait. If you are the headline act then you may have done your sound check at 6pm, but your stage time isn't till 10.30pm, so you have over four hours to wait.

Try to find somewhere to relax. Some venues have band rooms backstage where you can chill out. Use this time to make sure your instruments are all set up properly and run through the set with the band if you need to, making sure everyone knows what you are going to be playing. Singers might do some vocal exercises, you might feel a bit silly doing this especially in front of people, but it really helps; you want your voice to be warmed up and ready to go from the first word you sing.

Try to avoid getting drunk! Perhaps a pint before you go on will help your nerves, but drink any more than this and it will affect your playing ability and you don't want that.

We once did a Cujo gig at Turnmills in London. It was my birthday so I decided to get someone else to drive so I could have a few beers. It wasn't a good idea. Not only did I play a terrible set, I fell off the side of the stage! Luckily I wasn't hurt, I didn't damage my guitar, and everyone found it highly amusing. Kevin then got the audience to sing happy birthday to me, which was a weird experience!

Before any gig, you want to make sure all your instruments and equipment is working, so do this at home or at rehearsal before the gig.

If you are having problems with your guitar, like the strings are too far away from the neck, or when you play notes up the top end of the neck they sound out of tune; then you need your guitar setting up. You can get this done at most guitar shops, or by a guitar luthier. But it's not too difficult to do yourself.

I recently learnt how to set up a guitar properly, something I wish I had learnt many years ago. I recently wrote an article on this for a website, and if you don't know how to do this, you will find the article very handy, so I have including that article at the back of this book.

PLAYING LIVE

It is important to work out a good set list prior to the gig. You want to spread out your best songs: one at the beginning, one at the end, and the rest spread throughout. Split up songs that are in the same key, and songs that are of a similar tempo. The audience can start to get a little bored if you play a load of similar sounding songs in a row.

Write out or print off a copy of the set list for everyone in the band. Sometimes the promoter or sound engineer require a copy, so always print out an extra one just in case.

About 10 minutes before your set time, make sure you gather your band together near the stage ready to go on. There will probably be a gap of about 10 - 15 minutes between each band.

If there is a band on before you, you need to wait for them to pack up and get their gear off the stage. As soon as they are off the stage, get your equipment on stage and set up as quick as you can.

Put your set-list on the floor in front of you, or somewhere you can read it easily. Make sure you keep it out of arm's length of the audience. I've had a few set lists pinched by drunk people in the past, which is pretty annoying, especially if you have made notes on it!

Only have a set list on stage, you can make some notes on it if you need to. Don't bring sheets and sheets of lyrics or music, it's important to know everything off-by-heart. You won't play as well if you are reading from bits of paper, and you won't be able to perform them with confidence and emotion, which is important. It also doesn't look very professional either, especially when you are playing your own songs. Also you will probably have bright stage lights shining in your face when you are on stage, and everything else might be in darkness. So be prepared as you may not be able to see any notes you have written down.

The sound engineer will be on stage to help bands get set up. Once everything is plugged in and set up, the engineer will then go back to his desk and ask you if you are ready to start. They might speak to you from the desk, through a microphone - which comes out your monitor speaker, or they might just give you a thumbs up; so make sure you keep an eye on what the engineer is doing. If you are ready, give them a thumbs up back and they will turn the PA speakers on so everyone can hear you and you can start your set!

You can either go straight into your first song, or you could speak to the audience and introduce the band. Speaking to the audience is the job of your lead singer, but anyone with a microphone can too. Make sure you mention your bands name during the gig, and also your website address. You need to make sure everyone at the gig knows who they are listening to.

After you have played a song, make sure you let the last note ring out nicely, and if the audience are applauding, let that go on for a few seconds. After that you need to either speak to the audience, or go into your next song.

Some people are naturally good at speaking to the audience, they can always think of great things to say, on the spot. Some people, like me, are not so good at this. If you are like me, it's good to plan a few things you might say, prior to the gig. If you can't think of anything you might say, go on YouTube and watch some live performances of your favorite bands, listen to what they say between songs and get some ideas.

You will probably be quite nervous before and during a gig, especially for your first few. This is perfectly normal; loads of famous, very experienced artists get nervous before going on stage. Just remember, if you are well rehearsed, then you are going to sound great!

If I get nervous on stage, perhaps we're about to play a new song for the first time, or were about to play a song that I find quite difficult to play; I try and ignore the crowd and pretend I'm playing in the rehearsal room and just concentrate on what I'm playing, I find this helps.

If you do make a mistake during song, just carry on; chances are the audience won't even notice. Usually the only way the crowd will know you've cocked something up is if you look like you've just cocked something up! So if you just carry on, they might notice something didn't sound quite right for a millisecond, but they probably won't know why or who it was, or they won't notice at all.

Have an emergency song or jam worked out in case something goes wrong, like the snare skin breaking, or a guitar/bass string breaking, or an amp blowing. The audience will get very bored if you're all standing around waiting for someone to fix something.

In Cujo we had a couple of acoustic songs that Kevin would play if Jamie or I had to fix something, change a string, or a drum skin or something. If Kevin broke a string and had to get his spare guitar plugged in or change a string, Jamie and I would play a drum and bass jam. We might jam around the intro of the next song, so when Kevin is ready he can join in and we can go straight into the next song.

Guitarists - make sure you have a spare guitar set up and tuned and ready to go if you break a string; or if you don't own another guitar, make sure you have everything you need to change a string very quickly. The quickest way to do this is to have a pair of wire cutters/pliers, spare stings and a string winder. Rip the broken string off, thread a new one and use the winder to tighten it up quickly, then cut the excess off with the wire cutters.

Don't tune guitars whilst the guitar is amplified, and buy yourself a decent foot pedal tuner. I've had many different tuners over the years, but a couple of years ago I bought a guitar pedal tuner and I love it, best tuner I've ever had. It's just like an effects pedal; you plug your guitar into the input, then plug a second lead from the output into your amp. When you press the pedal it cuts the signal to your amp, muting the sound, and turns the tuner on so you can tune up, when you've finished tuning, press the pedal again and it unmutes.

I bought the Behringer TU300. I may upgrade to the Boss TU3 when I'm feeling rich. Boss pedals are more expensive but a better build quality, and the tuning sensitivity will be a bit better. If I sell a few of these books then the Boss tuner is what I'm going to buy with the proceeds!

Another handy item I bought in recent years was a fold up Guitar stand. I bought the Hercules iStand. I was always resting my guitar up against my amp, and always knocking it over, I'm lucky I never broke the neck! My new stand is great, my guitar is now safe on-stage, then the stand folds up and fits neatly into my gig bag.

Drummers - make sure you have everything you need at arm's reach, spare sticks especially. If you play quite hard, then it might be a good idea to have spare snare drum, so if you break the snare skin, you can quickly just swap the drum for the spare rather than have to change and tune a new skin.

Make sure you all take plenty of drinks on stage with you preferably water. You will get very dehydrated whilst you are playing. Don't put drinks on amps or anywhere they can get knocked or kicked over, especially near any electrical equipment!

Other things you might need: spare cymbals, earplugs, plectrums, gaffer tape, pen-knife, medical plasters, spare guitar strap, a torch, batteries, leads, amp cables, spare fuses for your amps and perhaps one of those drink holders that clamp onto you microphone stand!

PROMOTING GIGS

Timing is key for promoting an event. If you leave it 'til a few days before the event, it will be too late for most people - they will already have plans; if you do it too far in advance - people will forget about it. You could list your event on your website in advance, but you don't want to start your proper promotion 'til about 3 – 4 weeks before.

First you need to design an advert for the gig; you need to use the same design on all your online adverts and on your flyers and posters. You can design this yourself from scratch or you can find a cool image on-line. Make sure you don't use copyrighted images, or if you do want to use one, change the image so it isn't so recognisable.

Use a bold image that looks cool and represents your music. You want a striking image with your band logo on and a venue

WRITE IT, GIG IT, SELL IT, MAKE IT!

and date. Make sure all the text is clear and easy to read.

You will need to create a few different shapes and sizes for the various different medias. For a Facebook event you need a square image for the thumbnail images and a banner style image for the top of the event page. For flyers you probably want a rectangular image, possibly A5 portrait and similarly for posters but A4, A3 or A2 size.

Flyers and posters

Flyers and posters are the traditional way to promote events. Even though there are many ways to promote gigs on the internet, hard copy posters and flyers can still be very effective. On the internet, gig adverts and events can pass people by without them noticing them. If you put a flyer in someone's hand, they are definitely going to read it.

You could use exactly the same design for your posters and flyers, but obviously posters are larger, so you have more space to play with. If you have any good reviews, you might want to add one or two of them to the poster, or perhaps include an advert for an upcoming single of album release.

Don't put too much text on, less is more in flyer design. Just make sure you put everything you need on it: your band name, where the gig is, when it is, what time you are on-stage, how much it costs to get in, and any promotion; and don't forget your website.

Your text should be something like this:

Cujo

Live at the

Dublin Castle

94 Parkway, Camden, London, NW1

Thursday 24th March 2016

Doors open 7pm, On-stage 9pm

Entry £6 with this flyer

www.cujo2015.com

There are loads of print companies on line who will print your flyers and posters for you. For about thirty pounds you can get a few hundred flyers and a handful of posters printed.

If you are on a tight budget, you can print them yourself. When Cujo started out, I used to produce them very cheaply. I would design four black and white A6 size flyers on an A4 size page on my computer, then if I could get away with it, I would print a load off at work. If I couldn't get away with printing them at work, I would print one off and take it to a shop that does photocopying. It costs a couple of pence per A4 sheet for photocopying, so you can print off 100 for two to three pounds; then you have to cut them all out. So if you print 100, you get 400 flyers.

Be careful what you do with your flyers and posters! You can give them out, put them up in your car and house windows, on message boards in shops, supermarkets and music shops, in your school or college, and in the venue itself. Anywhere else, make sure you get permission, or you could get in trouble, like I did in Brighton!

I arranged a gig at the Pressure Point venue in Brighton. I had four bands on the bill; our band and another band from Enfield, and then two bands from Brighton. I went down to Brighton a few weeks before the gig armed with a pile of flyers and posters. I had been down to Brighton previous to this and noticed all around town and down The Lanes, there were gig posters and flyers stuck on all the lamp posts, on the floor, on walls, everywhere! So, I did the same, I put hundreds all over town.

A week later I got a call from the venue manager. He asked, "Have you put flyers up around Brighton?" I proudly said "Yes, don't worry about flyers and posters, I have put them up everywhere!"

Then he said, "Ah, you don't know about the new laws in Brighton then? You can no longer put up flyers and poster and there is a £50 fine for every poster! You better give the council a call!" I had put up about 100, so we had around five thousand pounds in fines to pay! I called the council and after a lot of groveling; explaining that I didn't know about the new laws and we were a poor unsigned band. They finally agreed that I could pay just one £50 fine and not the rest! So check before you put posters up!

A good way to get your flyers to new people, and people who would be your ideal target is to go down to venues when they have famous bands playing, preferably ones with a similar style as your band. Give flyers to all to the people in the queue waiting to get in, or stand outside at the end of the night and give them out to everyone as they leave the venue. Whilst you are doing that, take the opportunity to chat and network with these people, they are much more likely to go to your event if they have met you and you've told them about the event.

If you are going to a gig, then take some flyers with you, you can leave them around the place on tables and give some out to people. But be careful not to get caught as the venue won't be very happy about you advertising an event at another venue.

On the internet

Once you have created your design/advert for your gig, put it up on your website, and all the social media sites you are on, and create an event on your Facebook page.

Social networks like Facebook are a very effective way of promoting your upcoming events in a way that allows fans to gather and create buzz, ultimately spreading the word by inviting others. Invite all your friends on Facebook to the event, and get all your band members to do the same. Don't be afraid to ask your followers/friends to help, ask them to invite all their friends too. If all the friends of your band members invite all their friends, thousands of people are going to get an invitation!

If you are doing a particularly important gig, then you might consider spending a bit of money on advertising it. Facebook advertising is probably one of the best places to spend some money on advertising. You can target an age range (maybe 18 to 25), location (the town the gig is in) and set a budget. You could set a budget of £3 a day for a week. For a week at £3 a day, the most you will pay is £21, but you are likely to pay less than that. Facebook advertising is one of the cheapest major platforms to advertise at the moment and can be very effective. I will go into Facebook advertising in more detail later in the book.

Make sure you send out blogs and tweets about the event in the weeks running up to the gig, and if you have an email mailing list, send them all an email about the gig. There are quite a few people who just don't do Facebook, Twitter or any other social network, so emails are a good way to inform a few more people who might not have heard about it otherwise.

You can get you gig listed on various music websites. You will probably have one or two for your area, so get on Google and have a look, websites like MrGig or AllGigs, there are loads of them out there. Also, if you are playing at a well-known music venue, you can usually get your gig listed in the NME and other music publications. Go on their websites to look up the email address that you need to send your gig details to.

Invite the press

Invite your local newspapers to the event and any music publications. They may come along and do a review for you, but even if they can't come along, they may advertise your gig prior to the event.

Text and email radio stations, commercial and internet stations, you never know they might just give you a plug.

I used to listen to XFM in London (Now called RadioX) and whenever we had a gig, on the day of the event, in the afternoon, I would text which ever DJ was on asking them to plug our gig that evening and quite often they would.

Anything you can do to create a buzz and get the word out

there about your gig will help.

We tried various different things to promote our Cujo gigs. When getting flyers done I used to buy some A6 mailing label stickers and print a load of the flyers onto these stickers. I would then stick them on lampposts, in phone boxes, on cash machines, in pub and venue toilets above the cubicles - anywhere where they would be seen by a lot of people. Obviously a few of these things may be a bit illegal, so I'm not suggesting you should do them, but try and think of different ways to get your event in front of loads of people.

SELL IT

WRITING A BIOGRAPHY

You need to write a good biography for your band. You will put this up on your website and any social media pages you have, so that your fans can learn all about you, where you are from, when you started, who's in the band, how you met, what success you've had, etc. It will help fans connect with you and your music.

You will also need a biography to send to people who are going to review a gig or you music, perhaps a local newspaper of music publication. They will need to know some background to your band, so the easier you make it for them the better and the more likely they will write a piece on your band.

It's actually quite difficult to write a good biography, you don't just want to write the facts, you want to turn it into a bit of a story or magazine article, so it's interesting to the reader and perhaps try and add some humour too.

Here are two examples of a band biographies. These are both biographies written for Cujo. The first is an interview/magazine style biography written by Mark Beaumont from the NME. The second example is a factual/story biography written by Cujo and our Manager at the time, Will Anderson.

Cujo Biography – By Mark Beaumont

The greatest bands survive the hardest knocks. New Order, The Charlatans, Foo Fighters, Manic Street Preachers: all know what it is to rise from society's ashes and triumph against everything the Bumper Book Of Bad Luck can throw at you. They know that whatever doesn't send you scurrying back to the dole queue with your Fender between your legs makes you damn near unbreakable. And now, to their stout ranks, are added another soon-to-be-legendary power rock force. The mighty and defiant Cujo.

Cujo are a new breed of Britrock beast; a band reared on chunky lumberjack shirt 90s American rock but, unlike many of their contemporaries, with a distinctly British bite. Here is a band that won't be content to be the Limey Papa Roach, they'll not rest until Papa Roach are the Yank Cujo. And here is a band with a history that makes Bleak House look like Chitty Chitty Bang Bang.

Spring 1998, Enfield: London's northernmost cultural wasteland and possibly the least rock'n'roll town on earth.

All encyclopedias state that - discounting crap Thin Lizzy covers bands and Chas and Dave - no band has ever come from Enfield. But two 20-year-old barmen in the Rose & Crown on Clay Hill - Kevin Dawson and Ben Keep by name - were out to change all that.

They had Kurt Cobain in their hearts, Anthony Keidis in their loins and a drummer mate called Jamie Hook in their local HMV. Together with then-bassist James Norton they were Cujo, named after Stephen King's novel about a rabid St. Bernard because they were wild, slavering and impossible to restrain. Er, and because someone else was already called Carrie.

"We just wanted to be loud," remembers Kevin. "We were into Nirvana and grunge. Everyone has a certain idol when they're growing up and Kurt Cobain was my one. I was sixteen when he died, it had quite an effect on my life." Cujo grew up fast.

Within months of forming they'd knocked out a rough grunge-heavy demo and played their debut nine-song gig at Camden's Laurel Tree; a gig so earth-quaking they've since had to close the venue due to structural damage. Not wanting to level Camden too soon they settled into regular gigs in Enfield and tried to build a loyal local following. Seeing as though every rock kid in Enfield was underage they might as well have tried to build an underpass to Sydney.

It was while waiting for James in a pub one night in 2000 that Cujo received a phone call that would change their career - if not their lives - forever. They got a call to say James had been killed in a motorcycle accident.

I'd known him for, like, five years, says Kevin, but Ben knew him for seventeen years and Jamie knew him for twelve. Some bands just play together because they can play instruments or whatever but we played together because we were all mates, so it was a massive shock.

Did you consider packing it in? Kevin shakes his head. James wouldn't have wanted us to. We'd done so much work. Such a sudden tragedy so early in a career would have destroyed weaker, less talented bands. But it gave Cujo new fire. Suddenly they weren't just doing it for themselves, they were doing it for James. A lot of bands expect it to fall in their lap, says Kevin. They'll send in a tape and it won't get put in a box.

Whole reams of songs were scrapped, new bassists were tried but found unable to fill the space and so, now as a three-piece, Cujo started again with Ben switching from guitar to bass and pumped full of renewed determination. Within the space of two years they recorded two full demo albums in Sonic One in Wales: the revelatory rock monster 'Can Your Grandaddy Do This?' (2001) and the riff frenzy of 'I'm Gonna Be An Astronaut' (2002) (It's like when you're a kid and you think you can do anything, the reality hasn't hit yet, you still think anything's possible. It was basically us saying 'we're gonna be a band'.). These were recordings brimming with brash rock confidence and melodic nous that recalled Nirvana, Ash and Feeder, yet with a sonic inventiveness

The songs cover all bases from September 11th paranoia ('Chemical Rain') to maudlin rock odes to being so pissed you can't get out of the middle of the road ('I Can't Stand Up'). From diatribes against New Labour to ramalama trucker-speed stormers called, ahem, 'Pink Eyes' (It's about a man going out with an albino girl. It's never happened to me though. I'm waiting for the day). Any one of them was fantastic enough to catapult Cujo onto a major label High Priority schedule but, uncannily, it was their upbeat tribute to James that had the industry flocking like flies to Badly Drawn Boy.

'Dear James' is a song we played live twice, says Kevin, but we didn't want it to become a song that didn't mean anything because we played it so often. The second time I nearly couldn't sing it. So I thought I wanted to write a happy song about James, which is what he'd prefer, and that's how 'Summer Song' came about. The verses are saying that we've been through the hard grieving bit and now we've got to be positive and the chorus is directed at James, wherever he is now, telling him to have fun. I don't necessarily want people to hear it and know it's about someone who's died. The weird thing is that's the song that got us on XFM and an advert with Pepe Jeans.

Yup, you read it right, Cujo have already bagged a jeans commercial, running from the end of July to mid-August on MTV Europe. Are you lot selling out already? No, when you've got bands who are already known and they do an advert, that's selling out. But this might be the best chance. And anyway, when Britney Spears advertises Pepsi it's her face that sells it because people know who she is. Seeing as no-one knows of Cujo yet, it's not us selling the product. It's just a platform to get us heard.

And sure enough, their music has proved addictive enough on its own. The Pixie-fied pop of 'Summer Song' saw Cujo picked up by Claire Sturgess on the XFM unsigned show the day after Kevin sent it in, and then selected to tour Spain on a hotly-tipped Unsigned Tour with soulmates Ninkasi (now split), Electric Shocks and Coin-Op this September.

After four years of lurking in shadows, Cujo are finally about to pounce. There's a buzz starting up, Kevin smiles, things are starting to click. We've worked our arses off ad now it's starting to pay off. In the past year guitar bands are coming back again but before that there was such a load of manufactured shit. We'd get annoyed with people getting on the telly, singing twice and getting a Number One with someone else's song.

If anything on earth were going to stop Cujo it'd have stopped them by now. They'll never surrender, looks like you'll have to........

Cujo Biography – by Cujo and Will Anderson

2005 sees Cujo enter its 8th year. Eight years is a long time and a lot has happened since the band's inception. In May 1998, Kevin Dawson (guitarist/singer) and Ben Keep (then guitarist/now bassist) met whilst working in a country pub together. Both wanted to start a band. On bass, they enlisted mutual friend James Norton and on drums, another local, Jamie Hook. Cujo was born.

Cujo hail from Enfield, north London, a place most famous for Chas 'n' Dave and the first hole in the wall bank machine in the UK, not exactly the most inspiring of histories! But, with panache and resolve and influences ranging from Nirvana and the Pixies to the Chilli Peppers and Queen, Cujo set out to change things. Unbeknown to them however, a tragic event lay just around the corner which would change their lives forever.

On July 14th 2000, Ben waited for a call from James to let him know plans for the weekend. Instead, he received a call saying that James had been killed in a motorbike accident.

In the immediate aftermath of the accident, the band was put completely on hold. Four ambitious and highly talented young men had become just three and the thought of picking up instruments could not have been further from their minds. With time though, life began to regain some semblance of normality and they decided to try and start up the band again, knowing also that this is what James would have wanted. So, with a new fire burning in their bellies, they grabbed their instruments and started anew with Ben taking up the bass.

After the low-budget demo of Big Muff Pie in December 2000, Cujo travelled to Wales to record Can Your Grandaddy Do This?, a nine-tracker recorded, mixed and mastered in just 2 days. The band began to up the ante on the gig front, regularly playing the London circuit including well-known venues such as the Bull & Gate and Hope & Anchor and within months they were back in the studio recording the follow-up to Grandaddy, I'm Gonna Be An Astronaut.

In January 2002, Cujo sent one of their tracks, Summer Song (a tribute to James), to Claire Sturgess at XFM Unsigned. The track was aired the very next night. Having heard the track on the radio, Pepe Jeans then contacted Cujo asking to use Summer Song, rather appropriately, in a summer-long pan-European MTV campaign. Seeing this as great exposure for their music, Cujo agreed and Summer Song proceeded to blast its way into millions of homes across Europe .

By now, Cujo were really coming into their own. They were playing bigger and better venues and were continuing to fight against the image-driven bilge that had become much of British and American music. In March 2003, Pepe Jeans showcased four bands at London's Camden Barfly with a view to taking them out to play in Spain (which Cujo did in July of that year). Playing on the same night were a then unknown Razorlight and Aussie rockers Jet, so by the time Cujo took to the stage at 11.30pm the room was bursting at the seams with rock-hungry punters. In 25 minutes, the band blasted out 10 of their loudest and meanest, working the crowd into an absolute frenzy.

Later in 2003, Cujo returned to Wales once again to record their most adventurous record yet. Ginormous saw Cujo progress further than ever before both lyrically and sonically. From the fast paced rowdiness of Fake Lunar Landing and Pink Eyes (a love story between a man and an albino girl) to fantasy tale of revenge on authority in Walk All Over You and the anti-ladism ode of Leave Me Here Alone, Cujo began to realise they were not just another garage band with a bunch of mediocre tunes. They were now a tight, well-rehearsed 3-piece with some blinding songs that would not appear out of place on any national radio station.

With this new found confidence in both their own ability and their music, Cujo began to gain momentum in 2004 and soon found themselves gigging more extensively and further afield with sets at London's Cargo and Camden Underworld amongst other established venues. In May, Cujo entered the studio once again and recorded ten new tracks. Six of these appeared on AlieNation, the band's debut commercial EP which was self-released by the band in September and has, without any record label backing, sold several hundred copies to date. In the same month as the release of their EP, Cujo were invited to play at the internationally renowned In The City music convention in Manchester where they supported The Subways.

Now, in 2005, and things look to be shaping up nicely for Cujo. They already have appearances at the XFM Outbreak Festival and the infamous London club night, Get Loaded (where they supported the likes of Shaun Ryder, Mani and Clint Boon) under their belt. They'll also be going into the studio this summer to record a number of new tracks with a view to releasing a single later in the year and have been picked up by one of the UK's leading music law firms. Quite how Cujo can remain unsigned after eight years is anyone's guess but, the way things are shaping up that looks set to change soon.

WRITING A PRESS RELEASE

You will also need to write a press release. The press release is similar to your biography but shorter and snappier, focusing on the points that will grab the attention of the press.

Radio Stations, Music Publications, Newspapers, Music Retailers, etc. will be receiving demo's and invitations to gigs and press releases from tons of bands, artists and record companies every day, so you need yours to stand out and sound amazing.

Be honest in your press release and don't be too cocky. Write it like something you would read in a magazine, just in black and white with perhaps a colour photo. Don't forget to include your contact details.

Below is an example of a press release. The below release was written by Cujo's Manager at the time, Will Anderson.

This press release was sent out with our single 'Do You Know What It Means?" press prior to the release date.

Cujo Press Release 2006

"...growly popsters Cujo are lashing meaty Ash riffs to Green Day punk... sheer Nirvana brilliance... it'll kill The Black Velvets..." (NME)

"Loving this energetic tune; the sand-paper vocals and punky guitars make it the perfect fast-drive soundtrack" (Notion Magazine)

"I was utterly blown away by how utterly f'ing good they are" (Glasswerk.co.uk)

"Cujo are the finest Ameripunk I've heard all month – 3.75/5" (Juice Magazine)

"AlieNation is an excellent album" (Cargo, London)

"This record is proof - Cujo are set to explode into the big time, and it may happen sooner than you think" (The National Student)

"Cujo are simply brilliant… this is the band you've all been waiting for" (Rhythm & Booze)

Unsigned Artist Of The Week – KarmaDownload.com (May 2005)

Winners of London Tonight/O2 Wireless Festival Unsigned competition / played the O2 Wireless Festival Nokia Raw Stage (June 2005)

Winners of Lee Jeans Unsigned competition (June 2005)

Winners of Virgin Radio Xtreme Unsigned Faceoff / Playlisted on Virgin Radio Xtreme (November 2005)

"So guys, how should we go about pitching Cujo to the media? Should we tell them that Cujo have been together 9 years and, unbelievably, remain unsigned?"

"Probably not a good idea, you know what the music industry is like, when people hear a band have been around a while and still aren't signed they get all sceptical, doesn't matter how good the music sounds."

"Yeah, ok, let's leave that one. Well, how about highlighting some of Cujo's recent successes, you know, being made Unsigned Artist of the Week on Karmadownload.com, winning the Lee Jeans Sounds Unsigned competition, winning the London Tonight Unsigned Competition and playing the O2 Wireless Festival in Hyde Park and winning Virgin Radio Xtreme's Unsigned Faceoff, that kind of thing? Or maybe we could mention the Cujo track that was featured in that pan-European Pepe Jeans ad campaign on MTV back in 2002?"

"Nah, the MTV thing is too long ago and none of the rest of it really seems to matter these days if a band isn't sporting tight jeans, pink T-shirts and singing out of tune".

"OK, fair enough. So, what the hell can we tell them? Surely the amazing response the band have been getting from their sixty thousand fans on MySpace is worth mentioning? And the fact that they're #1 in the 'Bands With The Most Fans' section on Bandwagon.co.uk?"

"Hmmm… not sure… perhaps we should just tell them that ultimately Cujo don't care how people view them. We know they're not out to be the trendiest band in the world. They're not out to start a new fashion. And they're not out to create a brand new genre. The fact is they're just set on making incredible rock music. No, they're not making the angular pop-punk currently sweeping the nation but the fact remains that the songs are brilliant and stand up to any signed act out there, indie or major."

"Tell you what, let's just leave it…"

Enclosed: Cujo Single 'Do You Know What It Means?' Scheduled for release on Monday 17th April 2016.

BUILDING YOUR BRAND

To successfully market your band or yourself as an artist, you need to build your brand. Like it or not a band or artists is a company, and to make it successfully you need to build a brand and market it like any company has to.

So what is your brand and how do you build it?

Your bands brand will tell a musical tale both tangibly and intangibly. It is the band or artist' character that leaves an impression on people. Your brand applies to every aspect of your activities, including your music, lyrics, performances, logo, photos, websites, posters, flyers, merchandise, etc. Even your social media posts, online interactions with fans, and clothing styles can impact your brand.

Logo

Once you have a name for your band, you need a cool logo. The logo is pretty important so try typing out your band in different fonts and different colours to get some ideas. There are websites that could help you find ideas like the free 3d logo designer picturetopeople.org. Make sure the look suits your bands style and make sure the words are readable. I've seen quite a few metal band logos where you can barely work out what the band name is which isn't good for branding! Once you have a logo you are happy with, use this same logo on everything you create. This is called brand awareness, if you use the same logo, colours and images on everything, people will remember you brand.

Photos

It's important to get good photos as this may be the first impression someone gets of your band. Amateur, bad quality shots of your band might give people the impression you are an amateur band.

If you or any of your mates are good at photography, you can do these yourself. Make sure you take them on a decent DSLR type camera, and make sure you do them in a cool location with good light. If you are going to take them outside, an overcast day is always good for outdoor photography, so it's not too bright.

Think about what each of you are going to wear for the shoot, this is also an important part of the design. Make sure there is a purpose to what you are going to wear. Try and wear something that suits the location you are shooting at, or the complete opposite.

Take a good selection of photo's: group shots, individual shots, close up, far away, landscape, portrait, etc. You will need to add your photo's to various different places so having a good selection to choose from, means you should have a relevant shot for anywhere you need to include a photo.

Once you have taken them, make sure you crop them well and try putting some effects on the photos, perhaps a subtle colour filter.

You also need great photos of you playing live. If you've got any mates who are good at photography, ask them to shoot a few of your gigs. If you don't know any photographers, there are also loads of photographers out there that offer live band photography, so I would recommend finding a few online and check out their photography portfolios and prices.

If you are on a tight budget, then you might be able to find a photography student who would be happy to do your live photos for the experience. You can contact local colleges, universities or adult education centres that hold photography courses. Ask for the contact details of the course tutor then ask the tutor to ask their students if anyone would be interested. Alternatively you could contact your local student union website to ask for help finding someone.

If you are going to get a photographer along to a gig to do your live shots, make sure it's in a cool looking venue with good lighting, ideally at a gig that you have a good number of people coming to.

A professional photographer will know what they need to do to get great shots, but if it's one of your mates, who may not be very experienced at this, tell them to get as close to the stage as possible, even on the stage with you. They will want to take shots from: lots of different angles, from the floor upwards, from up high, from the side, from a distance, some from behind so you can see the audience, etc.; with a flash and without.

Your photographer should take loads of shots. With the stage lights quickly changing all the time, it's impossible to know when the lighting will look good, and that will only last for a second. If they take loads of photos, you will probably end up with a load which are too dark or too light, but in amongst them you will have a few gems that took just as the lights were looking amazing.

Take photo's all the time. Take a camera to rehearsals, recordings, nights out, to gigs and back stage. You can never have too many photos. Every time you are somewhere cool, take a few snaps, you might end up with some really cool band photos.

Every time you get a good shot, post it on your social media pages. For your website you just want a small selection of really good photos, ones that suit the brand image you are going for. Don't overload your website with millions of random photos; less is more in this case.

Videos

Videos are a huge part of everyone's life these days, at the moment over 50% of mobile traffic is video. A decent video can get your band in front of millions of people.

A decent professional video is quite difficult to achieve on a low budget, but it can be done. You'll need one or two decent cameras, some editing software and the skills to use them. If you don't have the skills to produce a video yourself, my best recommendation would be to find some University Film Studies Students, who would be happy to work with you for free, or for a small fee. You might have to pay for their travel and for some video tapes or memory cards.

Your video needs to play out some kind of story. So first of all, you will create a story board. Your story board you can sketch out on paper, like a comic book.

What is the story? Listen to the track, read the lyrics, what is it about, how does it make you feel, what do you picture whilst you listen to it? Are the band going to be in the video, just actors, both? What should the location be? What are people wearing?

Your video will only be 3 or 4 minutes long, but you want to take about 30 mins to an hour of video so you have plenty of footage to choose from when you edit it together. If you are have the band playing in the video, make sure everything is in sync with what you are playing and singing.

Once you have edited everything together, try out different filters. Filters can make a huge difference to a video, just by adding a filter can turn a video from looking like a home video to a Hollywood film.

Make sure you include some details at the end of the video, your band name, the track name, your web address and a call to action. The call to action could be a link to where the viewer can pre-order or buy you track or album.

If you do want a really amazing professional video, and you have a nice budget saved to spend on it, then get on line and check out a few companies who provide this service.

Once you're video is finished, get it up on YouTube, Vimeo, Facebook etc. If it's a great video it could get shared millions of times. Remember the video by 'OK Go' for their song 'Here it goes again'? If you've not seen it, go on YouTube to watch it, it's a great video, very funny. The choreography was designed by one of the band member's sister and the band do all the dancing themselves, very simple and hilarious. This spread like wildfire and got fifty two million views on YouTube and got to 36 in the UK charts and into the Billboard Hot 100 in the US!

BUILDING A WEBSITE

Your website is very important. Fans, media, music industry, and anyone who wants to check out your band will go to your website. So it is essential that it looks professional, is branded well, is interesting, easy to navigate round, and includes everything visitors need to find.

These days building a website is pretty easy. You may know someone who can knock up a website for you. If not, there are plenty of web platforms that you can build your site on, without any knowledge of web design or code.

I've been using Moonfruit to build and host my websites for the past fifteen years, I highly recommend it, it's very easy to use and only costs around six pounds a month. WordPress is another very popular one.

Before you can build your website, you need to think about, and plan, what pages you're going to want on your website. You want visitors to be able to hear your music, watch your videos, view your photos, read your biography, your gig listings, contact details, latest news and links to all your social media pages.

Have a look at a few professional band websites to get some ideas, then sketch some designs on paper, or on your computer. Think about your brand, what colours and images you are going to use - what message you want to get out to people.

Platforms like Moonfruit usually have a load of website templates, so you could use one of those as a starting point to create yours.

You will need around 5 to 8 pages on your site and you want to cover the following areas:

1. Home page/Landing page

2. About the band/Biography

3. Photos

4. Music

5. Videos

6. Gigs

7. News

8. Contact us

You don't necessarily need to build an individual page for each of them, you can combine some of them on the same page, but you need to cover each of those areas.

Page Master

Once you have a plan of how you want your website to look, the first thing you need to create is your 'page master'. The page master is the images and text that are the same on every page of your website (unless you specify otherwise); for most websites this is typically a background, a header, a footer and the menu.

So what do you want your visitors to see, no matter which page they go on? Definitely your band logo, but maybe an advert for an upcoming single or gig, or maybe a quote from a great review you have?

You might choose to have a cool image for your background, then your logo in the header section, then perhaps in your footer you might put a banner shape advert on one side, then links to all your social media pages on the other.

For your social media links, there are two types of icons/links. 'Follow us' links; which if you click on takes you to the relevant social media page, or 'Share' links; which if you click will share your website on the visitors own social media.

You can find all the icon images you need on Google Images. Search for each of them, with the word 'icon', for example, Facebook icon, Instagram icon, YouTube icon, etc. In the advanced search section, under 'file type' select '.png' images, this will then bring up icons which have a transparent background (rather than an icon within a white square), these will look better on your website.

Once you have found and saved all the images and icons you need for your website, upload them on to your website and place them where you want them. Any image you put on your website can be a link. So for example, you would add the Facebook icon and under the settings for that image, you would insert the web address for your bands Facebook page. Then when someone click that icon, it takes them to your Facebook page.

Home page/Landing page

The first page of your website is known as your home page and is also called the landing page. It's called a landing page because when someone clicks on a link to your website or types in your web address, this is the first page they land on. Your landing page is the most important page on your website as first impressions are very important; you need it to look awesome and grab people's attention straight away.

Your landing page will have your page master design, but what do you put in-between the header and footer? Maybe some cool photos, some great quotes or a brief description of your band. If you have a great video, then maybe that should be the main thing people see on your landing page, or if you are promoting a certain song or album, include a large advert for that.

If you have some good write-ups from magazines, music websites or local papers, you should include these on your website, but you could use the best parts of them on the landing page. For example, Mark Beaumont of the NME did a short review of one of our Cujo singles. The review read:

"The Suburbs, how bountiful your sounds,! While Staines is a-roll with hooded diska types attacking CCTV cameras with spray-on glitter cans, around the M25 in Enfield growly popsters Cujo are lashing meaty Ash riffs to GreenDay punk with the studio wires that made Neil Armstrong appear weightless in 1969 and invented conspiracy rock. I'd elaborate on the sheer Nirvana brilliance and how it will kill the Black Velvets, but two men in black suits just came round, showed me a torch and I can barely remember a thing about it now"
© Mark Beaumont/NME/Time Inc (UK) Ltd

We didn't want to write all that on our landing page or on our flyers and posters, so we cut it down to:

"...growly popsters Cujo are lashing meaty Ash riffs to Green Day punk... sheer Nirvana brilliance... it'll kill The Black Velvets..." (NME)

In any review you've had, even if the whole review isn't all great, you can normally find a good line or two that you can quote that sounds really good.

About us/Biography page

This page you need to include you biography, and anything else interesting about your band that your visitors would like to know. Maybe include you press release, or any reviews you have.

Photos page

Web platforms like Moonfruit have slideshow widgets that you can upload your images onto, which is an easy and effective way of presenting your photos.

Don't put too many photos on your website, maybe 5 - 10 band shots and 5 - 10 live shots. Make sure you use your best photos, good quality photos that fit the look/brand you are going for.

Music & Video page

Moonfruit doesn't have its own music or video players, but they give you an option to add snippets of HTML code. Using HTML Snippets you can add music or video players from other websites, these are called widgets. So for a music player, you would upload your songs onto websites like Soundcloud, and for Videos you will need to upload to sites like YouTube or Vimeo.

On Soundcloud, YouTube or Vimeo, go to the song or video you have uploaded and look for the share options. You will see an option to 'embed' on your website. This will generate some

HTML code. What you have to do is copy that code, then paste it into the HMTL snippet tool on your website. If it is a code from Soundcloud, it will create a Soundcloud widget on your webpage, with your song on it!

You can use HTML Snippets for various things. You could add a Twitter or Facebook widget, which would show all your recent tweets or posts, you could add forms that you can use for competitions or voting, perhaps a countdown timer that counts down to a single or album release. The option are endless. If you think of something you want on your website, and Moonfruit doesn't include it as a standard feature, then Google it and you're bound to find a few widgets you can use.

Gigs page

List all your upcoming gigs on this page. Make sure you add all the information people will need to know, including instructions on how to buy tickets. If you are selling tickets yourself, you could add a PayPal widget so people can buy them directly from your website.

Contact us page

Make sure you have at least an email address for people to contact you. You never know who might have discovered your band and want to get in touch.

Usually when you buy a domain name/web address, you get free email forwarding. You should take advantage of this rather than use your personal email address as it looks more professional. For example, when I bought www.cujo.cc I got free email forwarding. So I set up the email address contact@cujo.cc which forwarded to my personal email address.

It's good to try and capture the information of whoever visits your website. You can do this by adding a form that people have to fill in. It could just be a contact us form, or you could ask people to complete the form to be added to your mailing list, or you could run a competition to win something, maybe an album or gig tickets.

You can add whatever questions you like to a form but try and keep it quite short. All you really need is their name and email address, but it's also handy to know where people live and what age and sex they are. Make sure you save the details of anyone who gets in touch through your website, and add them to your mailing list.

News or Blog page

Most web platforms have the option to put a blog on your website. A blog is very important, this is where you can keep all your fans updated on latest news about the band. The more personal you can make it, the better. Get fans behind the scenes in the writing process, or post photos of you in the rehearsal studio or from gigs. Fans will comment on your blogs and you can comment back and build relationships with therm.

Shop or Merchandise page

If you have any merchandise to sell: CD's, badges, T-shirts, stickers, etc. you can add a store or shop page to your website. You can use the HTML tool I mentioned earlier to add a Paypal widget to your page so people can pay. You can also use the PayPal widget to sell tickets to your gigs.

Keywords

You will need to add 'keywords' to your site to help people find it on Google or other search engines. You should be able to find a section on whichever web platform you are using to add keywords. You need to add words that people are likely to type into Google when trying to find your band or maybe searching for gigs in your area. So you need to add keywords like: the name of your band, words like 'band', 'music', 'rock' (If you are a rock band) and the name of the town you are based.

Once you have built your site, make sure you test it. Go all over the site, test all the links, songs, videos, emails, etc. and make sure everything does what it's supposed to. Once you are happy everything is done, then you need to buy a domain name.

Web address/Domain name

The domain name is the web address people will type in to get to your website. There are lots of places on-line that you can purchase them, like 1and1, 123reg, Godaddy, etc. But if you are building your website on a platform like Moonfruit, you can buy the domain on their site. These are usually very cheap, about £8 - £10 for two years.

There are loads of different ones you can buy but ideally you want to buy the '.com' or the '.co.uk' as these are the most well-known and sought after.

Our band was called Cujo, so we wanted to buy www.cujo.com or www.cujo.co.uk, unfortunately the Cambridge University Jazz Orchestra (CUJO) had already bought the '.com' and '.co.uk'! In the end, we bought www.cujo.cc instead.

Once you have bought your domain, you need to set it up so that it's connected to the web address where your website is hosted. Once they are linked, your website is live.

If you've not finished building your site, it's best not to link it up yet, It doesn't look very professional if you advertise a website and when people view it, it's only half built.

When you website is live, make sure you announce it to all your friends/fans on social media and ask them to check it out.

DIGITAL MARKETING

Digital marketing is a vital part of your marketing strategy. These days you can do an enormous amount of promotion online and in many different ways. The amount of work you could potentially do on-line can be quite overwhelming, so the key is to get everything set up then automate as much as you can.

Social Media

Once you have set up your website, you need to set-up your social media channels and there are quite a few to set up, but it is well worth doing all of them. If you have done your website then you already have all the text, images, music and videos you need to put on your social media pages.

New social media platforms are popping up all the time, but the main ones you need to set up are: a Facebook Page, Twitter, Google+, Instagram, a YouTube channel, Myspace, and Soundcloud. It doesn't take too long to do, and you won't have to keep them all up to date individually, as I will explain a little later.

When I was promoting my band about 15 years ago we really only had Myspace and Bandwagon and a few other smaller sites. Facebook and Twitter were quite new and weren't as popular at . the time. The place to be for artists and bands was Myspace. I spent many, many hours developing our page. It had all our photos, songs, videos, biography, gigs, etc. It had a blog that we kept updated every day.

I learnt everything I could about Myspace, and all the tools that were available to cheat the system and grow your fan base quickly. I spent hours every night after work, speaking with fans and using a Myspace adder tool to invite more people to visit our page and listen to our music. I would visit the pages of bands in the same genre as us, bands who we had a similar sound to like Greenday, Nirvana, The Pixies, The Smashing Pumpkins, etc. then I would use the adder tool to grab the profile ID's of all the people who followed those bands and then invite them to our page.

When 'Bandwagon' came along, we were one of the first bands on it. I quickly worked out the best ways of building up our fan base on there as well. We soon became one of the biggest bands on there, we had more fans than most of the famous bands.

Bandwagon noticed this and started using our page as an example to advertise Bandwagon to other bands and artists, which in turn made more people follow our page.

After a few months, with all the different tricks and tools I'd learnt to promote our pages, we had over sixty thousand fans on these two sites, which for an unsigned band was a huge amount of followers; this gave us a huge advantage when we promoted gigs and singles/albums.

Things have changed now and Myspace and Bandwagon aren't the most popular sites any more. You have to keep up to date with the latest websites, software, trends, tricks and tools to help you build your fan base and promote your music. If you get into this and work hard to find different ways to attract people to follow your pages, you can build up a large following pretty quickly. If you have a single or album you want to release, the more people you can market this to the better. If you already have tens of thousands of people following your various different pages, you have a massive head start!

Facebook

Probably the most important medium these days is Facebook, roughly one and a half billion people use Facebook at the moment! Facebook is always improving their site and one recent changes was the option to build specific p companies and this includes bands.

You can add all your Photos, Music, Vi

(events),etc.; then invite everyone you know to visit your page and like it.

Facebook advertising is also very clever these days and quite cost effective. Let's say you have booked a gig in London but you live in Manchester and you don't have any fans in London yet. You can choose to advertise your gig only to people who are most likely to attend. You could choose people who live in London, of a certain age range, and like a certain genre of music.

Or you might want to advertise a singles or album. Let's say you are releasing a single in two weeks' time on iTunes; you could create a picture advert for the single with the text: 'listen to it now on iTunes!' You then create a Facebook advert, upload that image and add a link to your song on iTunes. Choose your target audience, when you want your advert to start and finish and what your budget is. You 'pay per click', so you only pay when people click on your advert. If someone clicks on it, it takes them to your track on iTunes. They can listen to the track, if they like it, they pre-order it! If no-one clicks on your advert, then you don't pay anything.

You choose a daily budget, so perhaps you decide you want to spend £30 advertising a gig; you might choose to run our advert for ten days with a daily budget of £3.

There are lots of options for Facebook advertising, and I won't go through it all in this book. So log-in to Facebook and have a ˗ at the different choices. Have a play, set a small budget and try a few out and see what results you get. If a particular advert works well, then maybe you should invest a bit more money on it.

You can also now sell stuff directly from your Facebook page; this could be merchandise, music or gig tickets. Selling directly from Facebook is quite new, so I'm still learning exactly how that works, but you have to add a 'shop app' to your page. There are a few companies who offer these 'shop apps' that you can add to your page. I have not tried this myself, so I can't recommend any companies yet, but you can find out more about this if you Goggle it.

Twitter

Twitter is another important site to be on, Twitter has over three hundred million Members!

Setting up a Twitter account is very simple; there isn't a lot to do. Add a profile picture, a background, a short Biography, links to your websites, and you're ready to go!

Now you need some followers. How do you get followers?

Well, apart from adding 'Follow us on Twitter' links to your website, your other social media profiles, your blogs and emails; you need to follow other people.

Follow lots of people and some of them will follow you back.

Twitter has rules you need to abide by regarding following and un-following people, and if you abuse these rules you will get a warning, if you abuse them again your account will be deleted and you will have to start again from scratch.

There are a lot of Twitter accounts or adverts on the web that advertise that they will get you thousands of followers. Be very wary of these, you want the people who follow you to be genuinely interested in your band and your music, a lot of these services can get you a load of followers, at a cost, and most of these followers won't be potential fans, or even real people!

I have built up a few Twitter accounts which have thousands of followers, it does takes a bit of time.

I visit the Twitter pages of similar bands to ours, or pages like the NME, Melody Maker or Kerrang and view their list of followers. I go through these lists and follow all these people. People at the top of the list are the people who most recently followed these pages, so I would follow perhaps the top 100 people. I skip people who haven't added a profile picture as these people probably don't use Twitter that much. You really want active Twitter users as you want these people to read your Tweets and most importantly like or re-tweet.

Once you have followed 2,000 people you hit the first Twitter limit. You will not be able to follow any more until you get a load of people following you back. This limit will increase once you have more followers. I'm not sure what the ratio is, but it's something like: once you have 1,500 people following you, then your limit goes up to 3,000.

Once you've hit the 2,000 people limit, you need to leave it for a day or so to give people a chance to notice that you have followed them, and follow you back. A lot of people won't follow you back so you need to un-follow them so you can follow more people. This is where it gets dangerous as if you unfollow loads of people that don't follow you, Twitter sees there is something fishy going on and gives you a warning or bars you.

There are tools to help you do this, the one I have found to be best is an app called 'Unfollow'. What Unfollow does is looks through your account at all the people you are following, then produces a list of all the people who don't follow you back.

You can then choose how many of these people you want to unfollow. Don't unfollow them all at once or Twitter will clock on to what you are doing. I normally unfollow around 100 people a day, I'm not sure how many more you can unfollow before Twitter penalises you. After reading lots of threads online about this, I think only the people at Twitter know this.

Once you have unfollowed those 100 people, then you can follow another 100 new people. After a few weeks of this you'll start to build a good following.

Building your followers is only half of it. You do need to be regularly tweeting interesting tweets, or people will get bored and unfollow you. You don't need to do this from Twitter, the reason why I will be explaining in a bit.

Twitter also offer 'pay per click' advertising. It's not as clever as Facebook advertising, but something worth considering when you are doing a big campaign to release music.

Google+ is another site you need to add your details to. You might be thinking, "why bother with Google+, no-one uses it!" Well you should, for the same reason you should have a YouTube channel. Who owns YouTube and Google+? Google do, and everyone uses Google. And which websites are Google likely to put top of the list when people search on Google? Youtube and Google+!

I won't go into detail about any of the other social media sites as they are pretty self-explanatory. However, I should emphasise: add your videos to YouTube and Vimeo, add your songs to Soundcloud, Last FM, Garageband, add your photos to Instagram, Flikr, Tumblr, etc.; and make sure you add links between all these sites and your website.

AUTOMATION

Once you have set up all these social media pages, you need to constantly blog, tweet, post pictures, add comments, interact with fans, etc. on all of them. Sounds like a full time job doesn't it?! Well it doesn't have to be. This is where our automation comes in.

There are a few websites and apps that provide these services, but the two I recommend are Hootsuite and ITTT (If This Then That)

ITTT and Hootsuite do similar things, they do: If This Then That!

For example, if you set up a blog on your website, you tell one of these websites: If I post a blog on my website (If This), then automatically post that blog to my Facebook page, Tweet it on

My Twitter, Post it on my Instagram, my Google+, My Flikr, etc. (Then That) and it will! Even better, you can schedule your blog posts.

You could spend an hour on a Sunday afternoon, for example, writing blogs and scheduling them. If you can think of 21 blogs to write, you can schedule 3 a day, every day for the next week. Once that is set up, you will automatically be posting stuff on all your social media sites, 3 times a day, without you having to do anything!

There are certain days and times of the day that most people are on social media. If you think, most people are at work, University, School, etc. from Monday to Friday. When are people most likely going to be on their phones looking at their social media app?

It is most likely to be about 8am when they are having their breakfast; between 12.p.m. and 2.p.m. when they are on lunch or from around 6pm till 10pm when they are home from work, and before they go to bed. At the weekend statistics show that people are online mostly first thing in the morning or late at night. So think about when you want to schedule your posts to go out, you want them to be viewed by as many people as possible.

On Hootsuite you can also view the activity of all your social media posts. It's good to keep an eye on this: which posts have been most successful, which didn't work very well. If you had a particular post that got shared loads of times, then write more blogs like that one.

Set up Google Alerts. With Google Alerts, you'll automatically receive an email from Google, any time Google indexes a mention of your band on-line. This could be fans talking about your band on social media or music publications posting reviews of your music or gigs. Every time a good one comes in, save it, put it on your website, blog and share it.

BLOGGING

So what should you blog? Obviously you want to keep people updated on what's going on with the band, what gigs are coming up, what songs you are releasing, what radio stations ae going to play your tune, where they can view you latest video, etc. That's all important stuff, but if that's all you blog, people might get a bit bored of it.

Be real, have an opinion, tell stories, just like you are talking to your mates. You want to connect with all your followers on a personal level, and they will want to know more about you, more about what's going on behind the scenes of the band. Share articles which aren't about your band, voice your opinions. You want people to reply, share, start conversations and interact.

Message your fans; if you see someone has posted something about you band, or just something interesting, then add a comment. If you notice it is someone's birthday, then send them a birthday message. They will probably be chuffed that they received a birthday message from your band, and probably more likely to come to your next gig.

You want your posts to go viral. Going viral means spreading like a virus: someone posts a blog, it's a great blog so all their friends share it with all their friends, then all their friends share it with their friends, and on and on until it's spread like a virus all around the word!

The posts you write about you band, your videos or songs; probably won't go viral, unless they are particularly brilliant or hilarious. So what can you post that will go viral?

Have a look at what is currently going viral; what are all your mates sharing on Facebook and what are the most shared videos on YouTube? What do you do if something funny comes up on your timeline? You share it so all your friends can see it too. That post will probably be going viral, but you didn't post it yourself - you just shared it, so your fans will see an interesting post you shared, which is good, but you could do something much more effective.

Instead of just sharing, you post it yourself. If it's a video, go find it on YouTube and post it on your blog; if it's a picture, save it and post it on your blog. Once you have posted this, it will continue going viral like it would have done if you had just clicked share. However, the important difference is, when anyone sees that their mate just shared this post, it will say they just shared your post (rather than whoever hared that post originally). So if that post goes viral, all over the word and is seen by millions of people, Millions of people just read a post posted by you, they've just seen your pages name (your band name) and seen your profile picture (Probably your band logo)!

Breaking music news always get shared, so keep your eye out for bands splitting up, artists getting arrested or passing away, or, new album releases, festival headline announcements, secret gigs, etc. If you keep a close eye on the music press, when some exciting news comes out, if you discover this early and post it, it's likely to get shared loads and go viral.

Even better would be if you can create your own funny photos or videos that are good enough to go viral. What are people going to find hilarious or really cool and want to share with the world??????

It takes 7 marketing 'touches' before someone buys into a product. What does that mean? Well a 'touch' is anywhere someone comes across your brand (your band).

'Touch 1'
Someone sees a 'tweet' that mentions your bands name, but they probably won't pay any attention, or even know they've just seen your bands name or logo.

'Touch 2'

They go into a music shop where there is a pile of your flyers on the counter. Again, they probably won't pay any attention to the flyers.

'Touch 3'

They are reading the NME one day, looking to see if there are any bands they want to see this month, they might scan past a listing for one of your gigs. The name sounds failure to them.

'Touch 4'

A friend of theirs likes your band page on Facebook, they now notice your band name; probably starting to sound a bit familiar now.

'Touch 5'

Then they go on Twitter and a tweet passes them by mentioning your band.

'Touch 6'

They notice a friend of theirs is going to your gig, they are now probably thinking, 'I should check this band out!'

'Touch 7'

A Facebook advert pops up on their timeline advertising your new single, they click on the link to iTunes, listen to the sample, they think, 'yeah, I like this' and buy it!

So that's an example of what the 7 marketing touches means. It's a bit like subtly brain washing people!

Don't expect to send a few tweets out and the world goes crazy for your band. It can take a good few touches before people take notice, so use all the possible channels to market your band, and keep doing it, it will pay off in the end.

Things can change very quickly in Digital Marketing, so it's worth following a few Digital Marketing publications on Facebook, Linkedin or Twitter, or follow some digital marketing publications. If you're really into it, there are some great free Digital Marketing Conferences in London every year. I highly recommend going along to them as you'll pick up a lot of interesting and valuable information on the latest tools and tricks available.

EXPOSURE

Aside from getting exposure on the internet with Digital Marketing, you need to be doing anything else you can to get your songs heard by as many people as possible.

Enter competitions. There are usually a lot of unsigned band competitions going on each year. I'm not talking about Battle of the Bands competitions in pubs, I'm talking about big nationwide competitions run by large organisations, usually by fashion clothing brands. Have a look online, Google 'unsigned band competition' and see what you can find. Enter any competition run by a well-known brand as there is a good chance you will get some excellent exposure from it.

We entered Cujo into every competition going and we won a number of them and got loads of exposure at the same time. We were the Pepe Jeans band, the Lee Jeans Unsigned winner,

London Tonight (ITV News) unsigned band winner, Channel4 Music, Urban Outfitters, Virgin Radio Unsigned, etc. Our songs were played on the radio loads, we did gigs in shops, our tracks were used on adverts and we were even on the TV a few times. All this exposure was great for our band.

So enter them all, and whenever you are in a competition, tell your local paper, they will be interested in writing a proud article about their local band on their way to the big time!

Quite a few of these competitions are decided by public voting, so If you've built up a good following on all your social media then you can ask all your friends and followers to vote for you. Make it easy for them, send them a link to the voting page. If you've got a thousand followers, you are bound to get a few hundred people voting for you.

If you win a competition, you get prizes! When we won the ITV London Tonight Competition our prize was a slot at the o2 Wireless Festival in Hyde Park which was awesome. Playing a festival stage in front of thousands of people was amazing enough, but we also got free beer all day and back stage we got to meet some of the big headline acts like Supergrass. So my advice is just enter everything!

The companies running the competitions will usually put your song up on their website with links to your website and perhaps a short biography of your band.

You may have to give companies the right to use one of your songs for free, for their advertising. Some people say this is 'selling out', I disagree, perhaps if you're a well-known band who have sold millions of records and you sell your music to a company for an advert, then perhaps you could say you are 'selling out'. But for an unknown/unsigned band - this is just brilliant exposure.

One year, one of our Cujo songs called Summer Song, was used all summer on Pepe Jeans adverts on MTV and on the Radio, think how many people must have heard that! Pepe Jeans also put us on a European tour with 4 other unsigned bands. All travel, accommodation and food was paid for; they printed 100,000 Pepe Jeans CD's with our songs on and gave them out in all their shops, plus we got a load of free Pepe clothes! I wouldn't call that 'selling out'; I would call it great exposure and an enormous amount of fun!

Another way to get your music out there is offer it to companies for TV programs, Film soundtracks or Video Games. This is an area I don't have much experience with. (Our songs were played on a few Skate DVD's but that was about it). These are all good ways to get exposure, but you'll have to Google that one yourself to find out more.

Radio stations

Obviously you want to get your music on as many radio stations as possible, and as often as possible. Commercial Stations are quite difficult to get on as they have pre-chosen play lists, plus there will be thousands of bands trying to get their songs played. But most stations have a new music or unsigned show. So do a bit of research and send your songs as a CD or mp3 to all of them. Hopefully your will get listened to and played. We got played on XFM, Virgin Radio, and BBC Radio 6 just by sending in a CD. You could try different things to stick out from the crowd to get noticed.

I once went down to XFM with a pile of demos. I didn't really have a particular plan in mind but what happened was quite lucky. As I got to the door of the Capital Radio building where XFM were based, a group of business men were arriving at the same time; as they got buzzed through the front door, I just walked in with their group. I went up to the XFM reception desk and said to the girl behind the counter, "Hi, I've come to drop this lot off" showing her the pile of jiffy bags which had the demo's in. She gestured behind her to the post room and let me behind the reception desk. So I ended up standing on my own in a little room surrounded by pigeonhole post boxes with all the different DJ's names on. I'm pretty sure I wasn't supposed to be in there, I couldn't believe my luck! I also had on my back a rucksack with more demo's in and a load of flyers and posters. So I put a flyer and demo in every single pigeonhole, and put some big posters up on the wall!

Try think of ways to be a bit different. I did have one idea which I never tried but thought would be quite good: go and buy an enormous cardboard box, the bigger the better, perhaps one of those huge boxes washing machines get delivered in. Put your demo CD inside the box and post it to a famous DJ at the radio stations office - they aren't going to forget receiving that demo!

A lot of people email music these days as it's so easy and free. This means far less people actually bother getting CD's burnt and posting them, so you should do both. Sending your songs on a memory card or USB stick is also a good idea.

There are hundreds of Internet Radio Stations which are easier to get your songs played on. Do a bit of research on the internet and make a list off all the stations that play your style of music, their DJ's and their email addresses. Once you've got that list, send them all an email with your press release and an mp3 of your best song and a link to your website. Internet stations don't tend to have anywhere near as many listeners as commercial stations, but it's all good exposure!

Street teams

Once you have built up a bit of a following on your social media, you will be surprised how many people are willing to give up their time to help you.

In Cujo, when we released a single, I posted a question to all our followers, would anyone like to help us give out flyers to promote our new single? To our surprise about twenty people asked if they could. So we arranged a location and a date, and they all turned up! We split into two groups, one group at either end of Enfield Town and we spent a few hours giving our flyers out. We then did it again in Camden a week later, and they all came again. We hung out with them a bit, bought them some drinks and everyone had a great time. So not only did we get thousands of flyers out, we now had a great street team of very loyal fans who came to all our gigs, bought our albums and played them to all their mates, and shared everything we posted online!

Charity gigs

Do charity gigs, they are a good way of playing to new people and picking up new fans and usually getting a good bit of press in local papers.

Business cards

Print yourself some band business cards. Keep a few on you all the time. you never know when you might bump into someone big in the music industry, or potential new fans.

Merchandise

You can get merchandise with your band logo made up quite cheaply: t-shirts, badges, guitar pics, hoodies, hats, etc. All these things you can sell at your gig or give away. If people wear clothing with your band on, it's free advertising; spreading the word about your band everywhere they go!

NETWORKING

I've mentioned this already but making friends and networking is very important. They say to make it in the music industry, "It's not what you know, it's who you know".

I will give you three examples I've experienced.

Example 1:

When Kevin, Jamie and I were starting Cujo back in the late 90's, we started rehearsing in a studio in Barnet owned by a guy called Steve. There was another studio next door, it was bigger, had better equipment and was owned by a guy called Brian. We often bumped into Brian and always had a chat with him.

One day the studio we usually booked was fully booked. Brian next door didn't rent his studio out but said we could use his instead. We got quite friendly with Brian and started using his studio every week. We later found out Brian was actually Brian Nash from Frankie Goes to Hollywood! This guy had written some of the biggest No 1 hits we've ever had in the UK!

Brian always popped in whenever we were there, which ended up being pretty much every week for ten years! Every new song we wrote, we played to Brian. He would tell us if he thought they were good or not, and suggested things we could try to improve them. Quite a few of our Cujo songs have parts that Brian helped us with. He also gave us advice on lots of other things about the music industry: producers to use, good venues to play, good bands to listen to, etc.

If we had not made an effort to make friend with 'that guy from the studio next door' we'd never had known Brian.

Example 2:

Cujo once played a gig at the 'Lil Back Yard Club' in North London. Also on the bill that night was a band called Ninkasi. These guys were awesome, like a British Greenday. We chatted with them all night and became friends. A few weeks later, Cujo got the call from Pepe Jeans who had heard us on XFM, and they wanted to use Cujo for their summer advertising campaigns. They also wanted us to headline a European tour; us and three other upcoming bands. We got on well with Trevor, the Art Director of Pepe at the time and one day I said to Trevor, "Do you need another band? We played with an awesome band a few weeks back called Ninkasi, their music would work very well with ours". I directed him to their website to listen to their music and gave him their contact details. A few days later I found out Trevor had sacked one of the other bands on the tour, and Ninkasi were now coming with us! If they hadn't been friendly to us, I would have never have recommended them to Pepe Jeans.

Example 3:

Willie, the Singer of Ninkasi, knew someone who worked on the hospitality ticket office at Reading Festival. One day he asked if any of us fancied going to Reading with him. I said yes, and Willie and I went to Reading Festival with hospitality tickets.

The hospitality tickets meant we were back stage, which was a brilliant time to network and promote our bands. I put Cujo posters up advertising our upcoming release, and every day I put flyers out on all the tables in the back stage area. I got to meet and hang out with some of the XFM DJ's that had previously played our music on the radio, like Alex Zane and Zane Low. We also got to meet loads of different music industry people and bands like the Arctic Monkeys, the Stereophonics, the Libertines and best of all Dave Grohl from Nirvava!

So, if we had not become friends with Ninkasi at that gig at the 'Lil Back Yard Club' none of the above would have happened. We are still very good friends with these guys.

So wherever you gig, rehearse, record, hang out, etc. make an effort to meet people and network. You never know who these people might be, how they might be able to help you, or who might become successful.

RELEASING MUSIC

The music you have recorded is a collection of your best songs which took a lot of time, sweat and money to create. You only really get one chance to release these songs, so you have to do it right. For it to be successful, you need to put in as much, if not more effort into marketing it as you did producing it.

You have to plan a marketing strategy well in advance of your release date, but even before that, you've some admin to do!

First of all, if you are in a band, you need to have an agreement in place with your band mates on how any profits are split. I briefly covered this earlier in the book where I suggest you split everything evenly.

If you have recorded your music in a recording studio with a producer, he may also be involved in the profit share. Usually you would just pay the producer/studio a fee for recording and that's it, but you may have agreed some things with the producer, so that's something you need to check.

You don't really need to get a lawyer involved (though it wouldn't hurt) you can download contract templates from the internet. Download one of these, amend it to what you have all agreed on and get everyone to sign it.

Once you've got your contract in place, then you need to register everything. You don't need to copyright your music. In the UK, all original music is protected by copyright from the time it is recorded or written down in some format.

Do you think you have a good chance of getting in to the UK charts? To get into the top 100 you need to sell about 3,000 songs in one week, to get into the top 40 you need to sell about 8,000, and to get to number one, you need about 100,000!

If you think you have chance of making the Official Charts, your need to make sure your physical and digital formats are registered with the relevant organisations. This will ensure that all your sales are tracked and allocated to you. You will need to register your release with the Official Chart Company, but before you can, you need to have the correct identifiers in place.

For physical formats, CD's and Vinyl; you need a catalogue number and barcode for each of your physical formats. To get these identifiers you need to go to the GS1 UK website: www.gs1uk.org

For digital formats, you need an ISRC (International Standard Recording Code). To get these identifiers you need to go to the PPL website. www.ppluk.com

You also need to make sure your songs are eligible for chart release. They have certain rules like a minimum price you can sell your music for, or a maximum track length, etc. You can download the rules from the Official Chart Company Website: www.officialcharts.com

Once you have your identifiers, you can register your release with the Official Chart Company.

You also need to register with a performing rights society. In the UK you typically do this with PRS for Music: www.prsformusic.com. All the people who were involved in writing the songs (probably everyone in your band) should register.

PRS for Music is made up of two separate companies: PRS (Performing Rights Society) and MCPS (Mechanical-Copyright Protection Society). PRS collects and distributes royalties for musical works that have been performed or played. MCPS collects and distributes royalties for musical works that have been reproduced or copied.

PRS for Music collects all the royalties from Radio & TV Stations, Big Concerts & Festivals, Online plays from sites like Spotify, Apple Music, iTunes, etc. anywhere your music might be played. They pay those royalties to the relevant artists.

Cujo released a single in 2006. At the time we didn't really know about all the things I am covering in this chapter, which was a mistake, we learnt them the hard way!

We did register with all the relevant places, but we weren't thorough enough in making sure we had done everything correctly. We did all our registrations, our CD's were available in HMV, available to download on iTunes and a few other online retailers. We had a brilliant marketing campaign running up to the release date, we did a small tour round the UK promoting our music and had an awesome single launch party gig in London. The result was; we sold a few thousand singles, enough to get into the top 100 UK Charts!

But, we checked our results and we didn't have any! We later found out that we had sold our CD's to HMV seven pence short of being chart eligible, and something had been set up wrong with iTunes and all our sales were credited to another artist who once released an album under the name Cujo! The other stores selling our single didn't count towards the charts, so as far as the Official Chart Company were concerned, we didn't sell a single single!

We did eventually sort these things out and got paid for all the music we sold, but our chance of being recognised as a band who successfully got into the charts were gone!

In light of the aforementioned, go to all the websites I've just mentioned and read up on everything. Don't take what I have just explained as gospel because things change, they could change the rules about how music is released after I publish this book resulting in what I have explained being incorrect. Make sure you are confident that every step you are taking it correct. If you're not sure, give the relevant companies a call and check.

Once you are registered with all these places, you now need to get your music available to buy from as many outlets as you can. To be chart eligible these outlets need to be well known ones like iTunes, HMV and Amazon.

To get your song up on all these websites can be a bit of a nightmare and very confusing! The easiest option is to use a company who do this for you. Companies like CDBaby or Genepool can do all this for you. They do charge a small fee, but it isn't a lot. CDBaby is a very popular one, they can sell your music in over 95 digital stores and over 15,000 brick-and-mortar locations. Just go to their website, register your details, choose you release date, upload you track and associated information - it's all pretty easy.

There are quite a few of these companies out there; have a look at all or their websites and reviews and pick which one suit you best.

MARKETING PLAN

Once you have all the registrations in place, it's time to make a plan! First of all you need to decide on a release date, which should be a Friday. Earlier this year they changed the rules on when the start and end date is for counting the sales for the chart results. The week used to start on a Monday but now it starts Friday morning and ends Thursday night.

You could research on the internet the best month to release a song, but you never really know how many other artists or bands will be releasing the same week as you, but probably avoid Christmas time as you will be up against a lot of big hitters! Unless of course you are releasing a Christmas song!

You need to work out a marketing strategy that runs for a couple of months before the release date, so make sure you leave yourself enough time, at least 6 weeks.

Work out your marketing plan with all your band members, everyone needs to be involved to be as productive as possible. As an example, let's say you are doing an 8 week marketing plan to release a single.

Weeks 8 - 5

1. Book your Launch Party. A launch party is really just a gig you organise yourself, but you don't normally charge entry. You want to book a couple of other bands to be your support acts and hire a cool venue, preferably a well-known one. Not a huge venue, you want it to be packed with people, preferably sold out. You should choose somewhere where music industry/press can get to easily- preferably a large city, somewhere like the London West End is a good idea as a lot of music and media companies are based there. Make sure it's also somewhere you will be able to get loads of people along. If you don't live anywhere near a city perhaps book a coach to take everyone from your town to and from the gig. The Launch Party should be as close to the release date as possible, preferably the week running up to the Friday release date.

   Think of it more as a party, put posters of your single up all over the venue, perhaps decorate the place a bit, maybe give away some merchandise, play some games with the audience. Try make it fun for everyone there. Get someone to take photos of the band, on and off stage and take photos of the audience. Take individual and group photos of fans.

2. Create a large advert for your release on your websites home page, or you could build a separate mini-site with its own web address/URL. Include all the details of the single, the release date and launch party. Add an audio snippet of your single and links to places where fans can pre-order it.

3. Get a load of CD's produced and press releases printed off. Make sure you have updated your press release so it focuses on the single release and the launch party. Do your research and create a list of Radio DJs and Music Magazine and Newspaper Journalists, find out their email addresses and postal addresses. Buy a load of jiffy bags and enclose a short letter, a press release and a CD and get them all in the post! You will also need your song in MP3 format as you will do this all again by email, but not for a couple of weeks.

4. Book more gigs before and after the launch party, not in the same area as the launch party as you want that one to be packed.

5. Start scheduling all your blogs. You want at least one a day for the next seven weeks going out on all of your social media.

In amongst all our usual blogs you can include blogs about:

- The Single release date

- The Launch Party

- Details of the other gigs

- Where to listen to the single

- Where to pre-order the single

- Any reviews you receive

- Which radio stations it will be played on and when

Make sure you ask all your fans to help and share your posts.

6. Design all the merchandising you want to produce to promote your album and send it to the companies you have chosen to produce it.

7. Think about what to do after the release, if it's successful, do you want to release your album or your next single whilst there is still a buzz from this release?

8. Schedule your Facebook advertising, maybe just an advert for your single, or maybe a competition to win a bunch of stuff like gig tickets, the Single on CD, A t-shirt, hat, etc. Or even better, do both!

9. Chase up the CD's you posted out by email and telephone, make sure the people you posted them to have received them. There is more chance the will listen to it if you chase them up, and more chance the will play it on the radio or review it.

Weeks 4 – 2

10. To all the media and radio stations you posted your CD's to who didn't respond, send out your single again, this time by email. Also email it out to all the internet radio stations.

11. Create a Facebook event for the single launch, invite everyone and ask them to invite all their friends

12. Create a Facebook event for the Launch Party, invite everyone and ask them to invite all their friends

13. Put up posters advertising the single wherever you can.

14. Get you flyers out in venues and shops and at gigs.

15. Send your song to bloggers and ask them to review it.

16. If you did a video for your single, get it up on YouTube, and Vimeo, on your website and start inviting people to view and share it.

17. Set up a Google Alert with your band name and the name of the single. Google will let you know whenever your single is mentioned anywhere. If it's a good review, blog it!

1 week to go

18. Get your street team out, giving out flyers and telling the world how great the band and the single is.

19. Prepare for you launch part, practise, practise and practise!

Launch party

20. Play an amazing launch party gig!

21. Make sure everyone that attends the launch party knows they have to go and buy your single on the release date, or the week following.

22. Take pictures on your phone at the gig and post them online whilst you are still there.

23. Get someone to go round and take everyone's names and email addresses and add them to your mailing list

Launch day!

24. Don't stop, there's still loads of promoting to do!

    Keep networking online, keep blogging, keep going! The following weeks are vital to build those sales up.

25. Post news about the launch party.

26. Post the photos from the launch part and tag people so they share it.

27. Email your mailing list and all your social media friends/fans with links to where they can purchase the single

28. Keep track of how many sales you have, if you are doing well - tell the world!

29. Blog a thankyou message to all the people and fans who helped make the release a success

Two weeks later

30. And relax! Then celebrate!

MAKE IT!

CONCLUSION

So we're nearly at the end of my book and I hope it's been enjoyable, I've certainly enjoyed writing it over the past months.

There is a lot of work to be done to make it successfully on your own. You really do have to get into a business mind-set: plan everything, keep track of everything, work hard, and pay attention to detail! You might get a few knocks, a few bad or mediocre reviews, but so did most bands when they started out, just keep going and don't give up.

There is a lot of boring admin to do, and lots of marketing to do, but don't let it get in the way of writing great tunes and paying amazing gigs - because that's what it's all about.

Be confident, keep writing, keep playing, keep plugging away, the more you do, the better you get.

I'm looking forward to hearing everyone's comments about this book, good or bad. In a years' time I plan to update this book, so please give me your feedback: tell me what you think I've missed, tell me if you think I'm wrong about something. I want to know so I can include it in the next version and can give the best and most accurate advice possible to up and coming artists and bands.

If my advice has helped you build a great band and successfully sold an album or single, let me know, tell me your story, maybe I can include it in my next book.

You can contact me through my website: www.wgsm.co.uk

If just one band makes a success of their music because of some of the advice in this book, well, that would be almost as good as a Reading Festival Main Stage headline slot for me! There is a hell of a lot over-produced, talentless manufactured music out there these days and not enough decent bands and artists getting through. So please follow my advice, be successful, and fill those radio station playlists with decent music for me to listen to!

Write it, Gig it, Sell it, Make it!

Good luck!

GUITAR

SET-UP

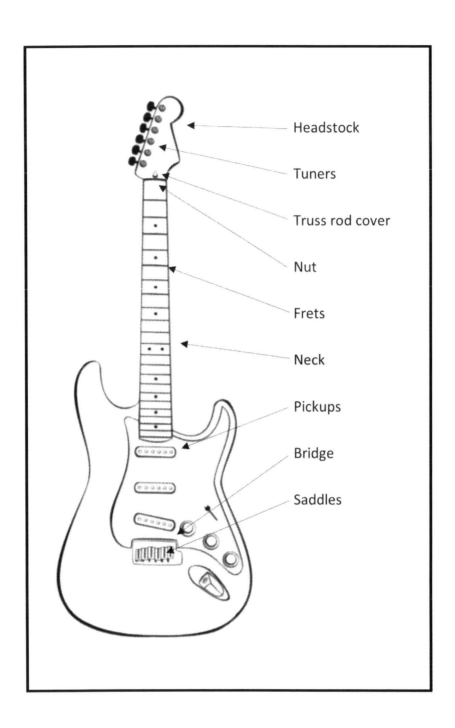

Headstock

Tuners

Truss rod cover

Nut

Frets

Neck

Pickups

Bridge

Saddles

ADJUSTING THE NECK

Tools needed: Allen key, ruler, screwdrivers

The first step of a guitar Setup is to check whether the neck is straight or not. The neck of your guitar should be slightly curved inwards, so the headstock will bow slightly toward the bridge. If your neck curves away from the strings you may have a problem that will affect the action of the guitar and you will need to adjust the truss rod.

The truss rod is a metal rod running through the center of the neck and tightening or loosening this rod will change the bow of the neck

Check the straightness of the neck for signs of twisting. Run a ruler along the length of the guitar, resting it on the frets. Do this on both sides to make sure your neck is not warped. If the neck is warped, you need to take to a professional luthier, or buy a new neck.

Hold the D string down at the first and last fret, then check the distance between the string and the fretboard at the 12th fret. Ideally, you should be able to slide a credit card between the D string and the 12th fret (approximately 0.10inches or 0.25mm). If the gap between the D string and the 12th fret is less than 0.25mm you will need to loosen the truss rod by turning it counter-clockwise. If the gap is more than 0.25mm you will need to tighten the truss rod by turning it clockwise.

To access the truss rod, remove truss rod cover, which is at the top of the neck just above the nut (Some guitars the truss rod access is at the bottom of the neck closer to the bridge).

To adjust the truss rod you need the appropriate size Allen key. Usually when buying a new guitar it will come with one of these.

Adjust very carefully using gentle quarter turns, letting your guitar settle between turns. If you notice stiffness when making your adjustments, you may be better off taking it to a professional luthier instead of risking damage to your guitar by forcing it. Once you have set the truss rod, leave the guitar overnight to settle before you play.

ADJUST THE ACTION

Tools needed: Allen key, ruler

The action of a guitar is the height of the strings from the fretboard. The string may be too high making it difficult to play, or too low creating a fret buzz. To setup the string height, hold down each string at the first fret. Use the Ruler to measure the gap between the strings and the frets at fret 12. Typically there should be 1.2mm-1.6mm gap between the fret and the string.

Adjusting the string height is done at the bridge. On a Fender style guitar this is done by adjusting the height of each saddle on the bridge with a small Allen key. On a Gibson style guitar this is done by adjusting the entire bridge.

Players with a light touch usually prefer a lower action, while heavy players prefer more height to prevent rattling strings.

SET YOUR INTONATION

Tools: Guitar tuner, Allen key

If your guitar is in tune but when you play chords it sounds out of tune, you need to set up your intonation. You can only do this if you guitar had a saddle style bridge. You correct the intonation by adjusting the length of each individual string by moving the saddles on the guitar bridge backwards or forwards. The aim is to make the open string note, the same at the 12th fret (but an octave higher).

Plug in a guitar tuner and tune the strings so that it is at the correct when played open. Then play each string at the 12th fret. If the note is flat you will need to move the saddle forward towards the neck, shortening the string. If the note is sharp you will need to move the saddle backward away from the neck, so that the string is lengthened.

On a Fender style bridge, the screws to adjust the saddles are at the back of the bridge. On a Gibson style bridge, the screws to adjust the saddles are accessed from the front of the bridge beneath the strings.

STRINGING AND TUNING

Tools: Tuner, String Winder

You should change your strings on a regular basis and always use the same gauge strings. String gauge is a personal preference. Most electric guitars come with light gauge strings (.009-.042). Most jazz guitarists prefer a little thicker gauge (.010-.046).

For strings to stay in tune, they should be changed regularly. Strings that have lost their integrity (worn where pressed against the fret) or have become oxidized, rusty and dirty will not return to pitch properly. To check if your strings need changing, run a cloth underneath the string then check the cloth for dirt or rust. If you find any, you should change your strings.

How you wind the strings onto the tuning pegs is very

important, whether you're using standard or vintage tuners. Start by feeding all the strings through the bridge and then loading them onto the tuners as follows:

Standard tuners: To reduce string slippage at the tuner use the tie technique. This is done by pulling the string through the hole and then pulling it clockwise underneath and back over itself; creating a knot. You'll need to leave a bit of slack for the first string so you have at least two or three winds around the post. As you progress to the sixth string, you'll reduce the amount of slack and the number of winds around the tuners.

Vintage tuners. For these, you'll want to pre-cut the strings to achieve the proper length and desired amount of winds. Pull the sixth string to the fourth tuner and cut it. Pull the fifth string to the third tuner and cut it. Pull the fourth string between the second and first tuners and cut. Pull the third string nearly to the top of the headstock and cut it. Pull the second string about a 1/2" (13 mm) past the headstock and cut. Finally, pull the first string 1 1/2" (38 mm) past the top of the headstock and cut it. Insert into the center hole in the tuner, bend and crimp to a 90-degree angle, and wind neatly in a downward pattern, being careful to prevent overlapping of the strings.

Make sure to stretch your strings properly. After you've installed and tuned a new set, hold the strings at the first fret and hook your fingers under each string, one at a time, and tug lightly, moving your hand from the bridge to the neck. Re-tune and repeat several times.

GOOD LUCK!

Printed in Great Britain
by Amazon